The Dominican Republic

The Dominican Republic

An Introduction and Guide

James Ferguson

MACMILLAN
CARIBBEAN

Macmillan Education
Between Towns Road, Oxford

A division of Macmillan Publishers Limited
Companies and representatives throughout the world

www.macmillan-caribbean.com

ISBN 1 4050 1021 5

Text © James Ferguson 2005
Design and illustration © Macmillan Publishers Limited 2005

First published 2005

Designed by Amanda Easter Design Ltd.
Maps by TechType
Cover design by Gary Fielder at AC Design

Photo acknowledgements
Alamy pp14, 62/63, 66/67(backdrop), 76(b), 92/93, 138; Art Directors and Trip
p56 (b) Art Directors and Trip / Ask Images p48, Art Directors and Trip / Helene
Rogers p65 (b); Corbis / Tony Arruza p59 (b), 86, 128, 130, Corbis / Tom Bean pp10,
55(b), 57, 91, Corbis / Brando D. Cole p61 (t), Corbis / Jeremy Horner p83 (t),
Corbis / Lawerence Manning p41, Corbis / Franz Marcmfei pp89, 90, 127,
Corbis / Adam Woolfith p87; James Davies Travel Photography p28; James Ferguson
inside cover, pp83(b), 80(t), 102, 139, 140/141, 143; Getty Images pp42, 50;
Hulton Archive pp7, 9, 16, 19, 23, 25, 26; Hutchison / Phillip Wolmuth pp27,
33(t), 37(t); Life File pp20, 26(b), 30(tl), 30(bl), 34(i), 51(tr), 134, 136; Lonely Planet
pp61 (b), 113(b), 133; Network / Laurie Sparham p30 (tr); Donald Nausbaum
inside cover, pp2, 3, 5, 6, 11, 12, 13, 21, 29(t), 33(t), 34(tr, br), 36, 37(b), 47, 51,
52, 53, 55, 58, 59(t), 65(t), 68, 70, 71, 72, 74, 75, 76, 77, 78, 79, 80, 81, 82, 83(b),
84, 85, 86, 88, 95, 96, 98, 100, 101, 104, 105, 106, 107, 108,109 110 111, 112, 113,
115, 116, 119, 120, 121, 122, 123, 124, 125, 147, 148, 151; Network / Ricard
Powers p52 (tr), 52/53(backdrop); P.A News / Empics p46; Topfoto.co.uk pp15,
18, 24, 33(b), 38, 49; Travel Ink / Abbie Enock p103; Zefa p112 (b).

Front cover : All images Donald Nausbaum apart from
Sammy Sosa (Getty Images).

Printed and bound in Thailand
2009 2008 2007 2006 2005
10 9 8 7 6 5 4 3 2 1

Contents

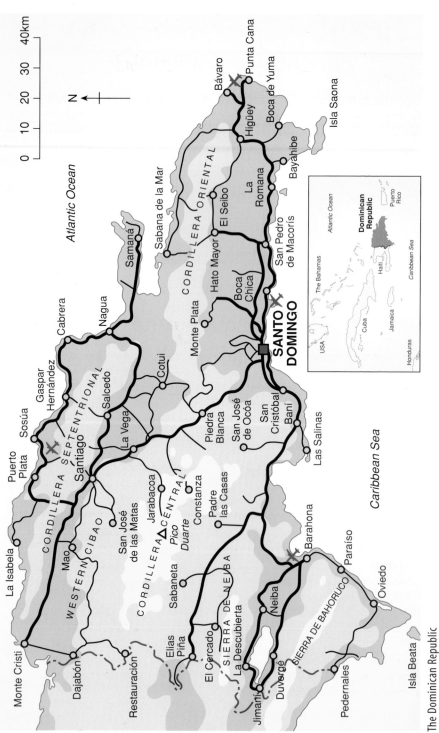

The Dominican Republic

Introduction
Where is the Dominican Republic?

Until the 1980s few travellers beyond Caribbean specialists had heard of the Dominican Republic or could place it on the map. If people in North America and Europe knew anything about the country, it was probably bad. This, after all, was the place where a pitiless dictator had ruled for 30 years. Even worse, it shared an island with Haiti, a byword for poverty and violence and famous for Papa Doc Duvalier and the Tontons Macoutes. Americans of a certain age would recall that the Marines invaded the Dominican Republic in 1965 to stop a civil war and to stop 'another Cuba'.

All these associations were hardly favourable to a nation whose tourist authorities have themselves admitted that its name is a problem. According to market research in the 1990s, the 'Republic' part was judged by potential tourists to sound 'too political'. As a result, the tourist board considered dropping it altogether and rebranding the country simply as Dominicana.

One thing at least is clear, however. The Dominican Republic is not Dominica, a small, undeveloped and English-speaking island in the Windward Island chain much further to the south. Indeed, the Dominican Republic is none of those things. It is not small, but covers 48 730 square kilometres (18 810 square miles), slightly more than twice the size of New Hampshire and bigger than Belgium or Denmark (it is 20 times bigger than Dominica, and Haiti, by comparison, has 27 750 square kilometres [10 710 square miles]). Nor is the Dominican Republic undeveloped, but boasts a large industrial sector, an extensive array of hotels and tourism facilities and a network of international communications. And it is certainly not English-speaking; Spanish has been the lingua franca since the arrival of the first European colonists in the early sixteenth century. And to answer the question 'where is the Dominican Republic?' the answer is 19°N, 70°W, some 960 kilometres (560 miles) southeast of Florida.

Part of the English-speaking world's unfamiliarity with the Dominican Republic has been a question of language. It has also been overshadowed by better known Spanish-speaking islands, such as Cuba and Puerto Rico. The long dictatorship of Rafael Leonidas Trujillo also meant that contact with the wider world was limited. All these factors combined to make this country *terra incognita* until the 1980s.

Then the tourist boom began. Suddenly, a mix of value, proximity to the United States and charter flights brought the Dominican Republic into view and within reach of the mass tourist market. Numbers of visitors rose steadily through the 1980s and 1990s, reaching an annual average of two million each year at the beginning of the new millennium. In response, the Dominican government and private investors, national and foreign, built roads, airports, cruise ship terminals and hotels. Whole areas of hitherto deserted coastline were transformed into tourist playgrounds within 10 or 20 years.

▲ Tourists on Cabarete Beach

Caribbean or Latin American?

Even today the Dominican Republic suffers from something of an identity problem among visitors whose ideas of a Caribbean destination are coloured by images of Jamaica, Barbados or the Virgin Islands. In many ways, the country can seem more Latin American than Caribbean, with its bustling cities, venerable Catholic churches and blaring salsa music. Soap operas – the ultimate Latin American passion – are also huge in the Dominican Republic, emptying the streets in the early evening. Some visitors can find certain everyday realities rather un-Caribbean. For those expecting cricket there is baseball; merengue is heard more often than reggae; rastas are unknown.

For its part, the Dominican Republic looks both to the rest of the Caribbean and to the mainland for its trading and cultural links. It is part of Caribbean regional organisations but it also identifies strongly with other Spanish-speaking republics in South and

▲ Bayahibe Beach

Central America such as Venezuela or Costa Rica. Certainly, its political system is closer to the Latin American model than it is to the rest of the Caribbean, where the influence of Westminster or Paris is strong.

But despite its Latin characteristics, the Dominican Republic is essentially and unmistakably Caribbean, but Caribbean with a definite Hispanic flavour. All the best things about the Caribbean are present here in abundance: a year-round warm climate tempered by trade winds, pristine beaches fringed by swaying palm trees, turquoise seas lapping onto white sands. Add to this some of the region's best rum, a cuisine that mixes Spanish and African inspiration, and music that has won international acclaim, then the country clearly has many attractions.

Its history, too, brings it close to the rest of the Caribbean, for the Dominican Republic has known the trials and tribulations of colonial rule, the horrors of slavery and the difficult path to independence. Its people have roots in Africa as well as Europe, and like other Caribbean nations, it has received immigrants from every continent during its history. In its architecture and art, its rural traditions and village life, the Dominican Republic has much in common with its neighbours, irrespective of language.

Claims to fame

But the Dominican Republic is also an exceptional country, a nation of superlatives. It boasts the Caribbean's highest mountain, the largest lake, the longest river. It also lays claim to being the first European colony in the Americas and as such has the oldest settlement, the first church and university, the earliest hospital. These historic riches, mostly clustered in the old heart of the capital, Santo Domingo, have been beautifully restored and are open to visitors.

It is not only buildings that make this country special. Its people have also won a deserved reputation for warmth and hospitality. In rural districts, away from the tourist trail, ordinary Dominicans are spontaneously welcoming in an old-fashioned way. To be sure, there are some in the capital and beach resorts who attempt to make a living from tourism and who are persistent in offering their services, but there is rarely aggression or bad feeling towards foreigners.

Individuals in different fields have also earned fame for themselves and their country. Since the 1930s many Dominicans, most from poor and underprivileged backgrounds, have gained legendary status in the United States as baseball players. Stars such as Sammy Sosa are household names among aficionados of the sport, and they have encouraged every baseball-playing boy in the country to dream of his own success. Music has been another phenomenal export, with merengue and bachata, the two home-grown styles of Latin music, spreading across the world through artists like Juan Luis Guerra and Wilfrido Vargas.

Dominican writers like Julia Alvarez and artists such as Jaime Colson have highlighted the country's creativity in the last few decades. Many other writers and artists are at work in a country that is sometimes poor in resources but often rich in talent and imagination. It can even claim to have produced a world-class couturier, Oscar de la Renta, who was born in Santo Domingo in 1932 before going off to make his name in Madrid, Paris and New York as a fashion designer.

It's your choice

What makes the Dominican Republic different in Caribbean terms is the sheer variety of landscapes it offers to the visitor. In no other island can you shiver in an early morning frost high in the mountains and swelter in a bone-dry, cactus-clad desert only hours later. In between these extremes are lush tropical valleys, filled with palm trees, high sierras where thick forests of pine thrive in the cool air, and fertile farming land, devoted to sugarcane, cattle or bananas.

▼ The River Chavón

Even the beaches are varied. For the adventurous, there are dramatic Atlantic breakers on the north coast, loved by windsurfers. In contrast, sheltered coves provide the calm conditions sought after by families. There are beaches for people-watching, where there is always something going on. And there are isolated stretches of sand where you will not see another human being for hours.

This, ultimately, is the real appeal of this rich and diverse country. There is something for everyone, from the tourist who is happy to stay put in the all-inclusive resort to the more curious traveller who wants to see some of the country's sights. Whether you're a sun worshipper, in search of an outdoor adventure, or keen to see Santo Domingo's colonial splendours, the Dominican Republic has what you are looking for. And that is why it is now firmly on the map.

▼ Beach life

❶ Written in blood
The history of a young nation

Gazing at the spectacular mountains, forests and beaches of the Dominican Republic's north coast in November 1492, Christopher Columbus felt a powerful mix of awe and excitement. The lush tropical landscape beguiled the explorer with the promise of unheard-of wealth and fame back in Europe, and his account of the island's charms was already filled with dreams of conquest and colonisation:

> La Spañola is a marvel. The sierras and the mountains and the plains and the champaigns and the lands [are] so lovely and so rich for planting and sowing, for breeding cattle of every kind, for building towns and villages. The harbours of the sea here would not be believed without being seen... on this island, there are many spices and great mines of gold and other metals.

Columbus' diary was in large part wishful thinking, written to be read by the Spanish monarchs, Ferdinand and Isabella, who, with financial backing from wealthy Genoese bankers, had sponsored his expedition across the Atlantic. They had risked underwriting the adventurer's audacious plans where others had refused, hoping to overtake their Portuguese rivals in the race to extend European trading links. But the diary was also wildly off the mark, for Columbus was convinced that the land he was looking at was some remote part of Japan and that the fabled wealth of China was somewhere in the vicinity.

Columbus had set off from southern Spain with his three ships – the *Santa María*, the *Pinta* and the *Niña* – on 4 August, hoping to find an alternative to the already known overland route to Asia and hence to bypass Muslim Turkish control of the eastern Mediterranean. The goal was the hugely lucrative source of silk, spices and other

▲ Christopher Columbus

goods, desired by European consumers but increasingly hard to import. The Italian-born explorer counted on making a personal fortune (he had negotiated a ten per cent cut of all profits) and winning the title of 'Admiral of the Ocean Sea'. He also had the support of the Catholic Church, which believed his assurances that he would convert any 'heathens' he encountered and hoped that any new wealth would bankroll a new crusade.

Unaware that he had in fact discovered a New World, Columbus remained adamant until his death that he had found the sought-after maritime route to the Indies. Hence, the name West Indies conferred on the islands of the Caribbean.

'In all the world no better people'

It is not known what the inhabitants of the island thought as they observed Columbus' tiny fleet approach their shores. Columbus had already encountered people on the Bahamian island of San Salvador where he landed on 12 October 1492, and they had wisely urged him to travel southwards. He had then skirted the coast of Cuba before arriving at what he called la Isla Española, the Spanish island (later corrupted to Hispaniola). Along the way he had been disappointed with people whom he viewed as poor and primitive, but still ominously remarked that 'with 50 men we could subjugate them all and make them do whatever we want'. On Christmas Eve, the *Santa María* foundered on a reef and Columbus decided to come ashore and found a settlement.

The history of the Dominican Republic is often recorded as beginning with this first makeshift encampment, but in fact its human history can be traced back about 2000 years before the arrival of Europeans.

The first inhabitants of the island are believed to have arrived around 500BC, having left the South American mainland. They were the Tainos, a branch of the people who had lived on the banks of the Orinoco River for several centuries before taking to the sea in their canoes. They moved gradually up the Caribbean island chain over many years, eventually reaching the large island that they called *Ayiti*, meaning 'high ground'. Why this great and perilous migration took place remains unclear, but it has traditionally been assumed that the Tainos were chased out of the Orinoco delta by another indigenous people, known as the Kalinagos or Caribs.

The Caribs were reputed by early European colonists to be aggressive man-eaters (the word cannibal derives from their name), but the people Columbus encountered in 1492 were peaceful hunters and fishermen, living in small settlements along the shore. These communities were ruled by *caciques* or

De Infulis nuper in mari Indico repertis

Infula hyfpana

▲ Taino / Arawak Indians

chieftains, supported by a council of elders. Living in large wood-and-thatch dwellings accommodating extended families, the Tainos farmed subsistence crops such as cassava and sweet potatoes, caught plentiful sea fish and hunted birds. They were a religious people, worshipping a trinity of deities: a male god connected to volcanoes and cassava, a female fertility spirit and a dog-like creature that protected the dead. They were also sports enthusiasts, playing a team sport on a special court with a rubber ball.

Although the Tainos lived in deadly fear of the Caribs, who were already making their way into the larger islands of the Caribbean, they seem initially to have greeted the arrival of the Europeans with innocent enthusiasm. Under their chieftain Guacanagarí, the local people helped the Spanish expedition salvage their goods and welcomed the building of a wooden fort, Puerto de la Navidad – Christmas Port – on their beach. Columbus was surprised that 'not a lace point' was stolen; later, he said of these eager helpers that there were 'in all the world no better people'. With such generous hosts, many of the *Santa María*'s crew volunteered to stay on the island and reconnoitre for gold while Columbus returned to Spain to organise a second expedition. Leaving a garrison of 39 men behind, Columbus sailed eastwards, dreaming of gold and glory. He had previously claimed the island – and its people – as the property of Spain.

The curse of Columbus

The idyll did not last long. When Columbus finally returned in November 1493 with 167 ships and 1200 colonists, he discovered the fort burnt down and its garrison dead. Another *cacique*, Caonaba, apparently tired of the Europeans' marauding, had ordered the massacre. So began the one-sided war between European and Amerindian.

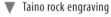 Taino rock engraving

Building a small settlement nearby at La Isabela, Columbus ordered parties of gold prospectors into the interior in search of the gold that obsessed him. Small quantities were found, but the Spanish were convinced that the Tainos were hiding treasure. As they grew more frustrated, and the Tainos more resentful, brutality replaced cooperation. The Spanish began to enslave indigenous communities, forcing them to bring fixed quantities of gold or face torture and death. A contemporary engraving shows Spaniards amputating Tainos' limbs and burning them alive. Tainos were put to work in primitive mines and either succumbed to exhaustion, despair or the European diseases of smallpox and influenza. When, in 1495, the Tainos rose up in revolt, they were easily suppressed by Spanish steel and gunpowder, and 500 were shipped to an early death in Spain.

▲ Ruins of La Isabela

The settlers also squabbled among themselves, with some despising Columbus and his two brothers, Bartolomé and Diego, for what they thought were inflated promises of easy riches. Many colonists were minor and impoverished Spanish gentlemen, unused to hard work and ready to act on their grievances. As dissent broke out, Bartolomé shifted the main settlement in 1496 from the malarial north coast to a spot on the mouth of the Ozama on the south coast. At first called La Nueva Isabela, this tiny outpost was soon renamed Santo Domingo.

Alarmed by reports of infighting in its distant colony, in 1500 the Spanish Crown sent a commissioner, Francisco de Bobadilla, to assess the situation. He promptly arrested the three Columbus brothers and sent them in chains back to Seville. Christopher would return only once more to his ill-fated Hispaniola, but his name was to enter Dominican history and legend. Even today, as his statue dominates one of Santo Domingo's oldest squares and the capital's grandiose modern lighthouse brightens the sky in his memory, ordinary Dominicans prefer not to mention him by name and talk of his *fukú* or curse.

Cradle of the Americas

With Columbus removed, the colony prospered, and a new governor, Nicolás de Ovando, oversaw the development of Santo Domingo.

▲ Early defences

Stone buildings replaced wooden shacks, and the town took the familiar grid shape of Spanish New World cities. From this tiny enclave, Spain expanded its empire: expeditions from Santo Domingo claimed Jamaica in 1509, Cuba in 1511 and Puerto Rico in 1512.

▲ Alcázar de Colón

But still the torment of the Tainos continued, with systematic exploitation of their labour and merciless repression of any resistance. By 1509, when Ovando left, there were an estimated 60 000 Tainos left out of the 500 000 alive in 1492. Their plight was worsened by the arrival of Diego Columbus, Christopher's oldest son, to succeed Ovando. He accelerated the process of genocide, dividing the island into *encomiendas*, feudal properties in which he and his cronies ruled over indigenous villages. As the Tainos died in their thousands, Diego built himself the impressive Alcázar on the banks of the Ozama. This symbol of personal power was soon joined by the structures of colonial authority and business: a hospital, a royal mint, a university, a building for the *Real Audiencia*, the law-making body for Spain's American empire.

Meanwhile, the Spanish colonists of Hispaniola were a law unto themselves, able to abuse their indigenous serfs with impunity. But as the Catholic Church established itself in the colony, so some of its spokesmen took up the cause of the Tainos. At a Christmas Mass in 1511 Father Antón de Montesinos preached a fiery sermon against human rights abuses, incurring the wrath of the colonists, who shipped him back to Spain. His indignation was echoed by another priest, Bartolomé de Las Casas, who wrote the massively influential *A Very Brief Account of the Destruction of the Indies* (1551), a damning indictment of Spanish cruelty in the

▲ Bartolomé de Las Casas

New World. These criticisms stung the Spanish Crown into reform, but it was too little, too late. The Tainos also attempted to fight back, but in vain. A revolt, led by the *cacique* Enriquillo, broke out in 1519, as he and his followers fled into the inaccessible mountains of the southwest. This rebel community was finally forced to surrender in 1533, and Enriquillo was 'pardoned', only to die two years later of tuberculosis. Ravaged by such diseases, the Tainos were effectively extinct by 1550, with only a few of their customs and words (barbecue, hammock, tobacco, maize) reminding us of their existence.

By then, a new workforce had been located in the form of African slaves. From 1518 slaves were arriving in their thousands each year, mostly to work the sugar plantations that had sprung up after Christopher Columbus had imported the first cane shoots in 1493. The first slave revolt was recorded in 1522, and the following year there were 20 mills in operation and exports to Spain of 1200 tons of sugar.

Decline and war

Despite its official importance, the colony soon began to decline. The small city was surrounded by vast expanses of undeveloped land, some used for ranching but most a hostile wilderness. The Church was a major landowner, as were pseudo-aristocratic families descended from the first colonists, but the poor had little access to land. Colonists continued to leave for brighter horizons; Hernán Cortés launched his conquest of Mexico from Santo Domingo in 1519. As the empire spread, so Santo Domingo slumbered.

▶ Hernán Cortés

Spanish neglect did not go unnoticed by other European nations, eager for a share of New World wealth and hostile to Spanish domination. Pirates from France, England and Holland began plundering Spanish ships and settlements from the 1530s onwards. Hispaniola's north coast was repeatedly raided, and the Spanish were forced to evacuate the city of Puerto Plata, leaving the area to the lawless crews of pirates and privateers who made temporary bases there. Even the capital was vulnerable; in 1586 Sir Francis Drake sailed unopposed into Santo Domingo, starting a month-long orgy of looting. Almost every symbol of Catholicism was vandalised by this fervent Protestant pirate. When Drake finally sailed away, the city was in ruins.

▲ Francis Drake

The Spanish authorities tried to defend their possessions, particularly the galleons loaded with Mexican silver that passed through the Caribbean, but could do little against well-organised pirates using the remote corners of their colonies as bases. The deserted expanse of northwestern Hispaniola was ideal for such a base, and it was here that, from the 1650s, mainly French buccaneers began to settle in large numbers.

Named after the *boucans* or pits over which they roasted wild pigs, these tough outlaws were a motley mix of pirates, deserters and other riff-raff who made a precarious living from raiding ships and trading meat and skins from the wild animals they hunted. From this unlikely beginning the French foothold on Hispaniola developed into a fledgling colony, with permanent buildings, trade links and even a governor, sent from France in 1664. The Spanish, confined to Santo Domingo and a few other settlements, could do nothing about this unwelcome competition.

An island divided

The colony that the French called Saint Domingue was finally officially recognised by the 1697 Treaty of Ryswick, which ceded the western third of the island to France. Spanish domination of Hispaniola was at an end, and the remaining Spanish colony remained an insignificant backwater. Underpopulated and largely uncultivated, it was a place of small villages and large ranches, with a sleepy capital city and a stagnant economy.

Saint Domingue, by contrast, rapidly became an economic powerhouse, exporting vast quantities of sugar, coffee and indigo back to France. Whereas the Spanish territory had few slaves (who were mostly employed as domestic servants or ranch hands), Saint Domingue imported tens of thousands annually, forcing them onto large and efficient plantations. The relaxed and ramshackle Spanish east was thus very different from the highly organised slave society of the west, with its irrigation schemes, burgeoning towns and fabulously wealthy planters.

Throughout the eighteenth century Saint Domingue boomed while Santo Domingo vegetated. Ships carrying cargoes of sugar, rum and tobacco plied the Atlantic towards French ports, returning via Africa with more slaves. Santo Domingo, meanwhile, saw few ships and little trade. What prosperity there was mostly stemmed from exporting beef across the border. But Saint Domingue's success carried the seeds of its own destruction. A small élite of planters and officials ruled a huge majority of black slaves and a discontented middle stratum of mixed-race *gens de couleur*. This society, rigidly hierarchical and oblivious to its own cruelties, was a recipe for revolution.

Revolution, occupation and independence

Saint Domingue exploded into civil war in 1791 when a slave revolt swept through the colony, burning plantations and massacring all in its way. For 13 years the conflict ebbed and flowed, as slave armies, French expeditionary forces and English troops struggled for control of the 'pearl of the Antilles'. The island of Hispaniola was caught up in the turmoil of the Napoleonic era, with Britain always eyeing the richest colony of its French rivals. The great slave leader Toussaint Louverture

▲ Toussaint Louverture

briefly ruled as governor-general of the entire island and sent troops into the Spanish territory. He was then duped and captured by the French force sent by Napoleon, only for yellow fever and lethal guerrilla tactics to win the day for the former slaves. In 1803, the year before Toussaint's successor Jean-Jacques Dessalines declared the independence of the new state of Haiti, the retreating French withdrew into Spanish Santo Domingo.

The Spanish colony watched events across the mountainous border with amazement and fear. Different armies marched in and out of Santo Domingo during this tumultuous period, but eventually the colony was returned to Spanish rule in 1809. Its neighbour, ruined by years of war, was now an independent republic, ruled by black former slaves, and the small Spanish and locally-born white élite dreaded Haiti and its territorial ambitions. At the same time, this native élite resented the presence of incompetent Spanish bureaucrats and dreamed, like others across Latin America, of independence from Spain. After several years of repressive colonial rule, a group of conspirators planned in 1821 to declare the independence of what they intended to call Spanish Haiti. They even contacted the Latin American 'liberator', Simón Bolívar, asking to join his projected South American federation. But their plot never took shape, as the following year President Jean-Pierre Boyer of Haiti led an occupying army into Santo Domingo.

The Haitian occupation lasted 23 years – a period often depicted by Dominican historians as their country's dark ages. In fact, the Haitians instituted various reforms, not least the abolition of

▲ Guerrilla attack by Toussaint's forces

slavery and the breaking up of the Church's monopoly of land. But the occupiers also ruled harshly, alienating Santo Domingo's mulatto (or mixed-race) population, who resented taking orders from and paying taxes to the black military authorities. Gradually resistance grew, and in 1844, the year after Boyer was ousted in a coup in Haiti, an independence movement called La Trinitaria spearheaded an uprising against the Haitian occupying forces. It was successful, and on 28 February 1844 the people of Santo Domingo found themselves citizens of a new country, baptised la República Dominicana, the Dominican Republic.

Strongman politics

This fragile new state, fearful of its more populous neighbour, was immediately weakened by infighting between rival *caudillos* (the Spanish term for local warlords or chieftains). The idealistic leaders of La Trinitaria, such as Juan Pablo Duarte, nowadays revered as the father of independence, were swiftly ousted by more ruthless and self-interested strongmen. Often backed by peasant armies that they paid out of their own pocket, these *caudillos* struggled among themselves for supremacy and dominated the country's politics into the twentieth century. One of the more successful was the wealthy mahogany merchant, Buenaventura Báez, who enjoyed five terms in the presidential palace between 1848 and 1878, printing money at will and plunging the Republic into debt.

Presidents came and went, often thrown out by peasant uprisings, as different regions of the country and their leaders vied for power. At the same time, Dominicans remained convinced that the Haitians would attempt another invasion (they tried, unsuccessfully, in 1849). This led the nation's warring leaders to look abroad for protection – to the US, France and Spain – and to one of the country's strangest historical events.

▶ Juan Pablo Duarte

General Pedro Santana, Báez's eternal *caudillo* rival, was convinced that the only way of fending off Haitian aggression was to shelter behind a European power. With this in mind, and with a plan to foist the worthless pesos he had printed onto the Spanish treasury, he invited Spain to re-annex the Dominican Republic. For some reason, the Spanish agreed, and in 1861 declared the territory a protectorate. This was the only recorded instance of an independent country voluntarily reinstating a colonial system of government.

▲ Altar de la Patria, resting place of Duarte

Yet the agreement soon fell apart. The Spanish refused to change Santana's pesos into valid currency and gradually whittled down his authority. Worse, they ruled with their usual incompetence and insensitivity, putting Spaniards into key government jobs in place of Dominicans and treating the mulatto population with disdain. Soon resentment reached boiling point and in 1863 a revolt in the northern city of Santiago announced a nationwide uprising. With punishing peasant guerrilla raids and an epidemic of yellow fever cutting through their ranks, the Spanish decided to pull out, leaving the Republic to a disunited local leadership in 1865. Santana, perhaps wisely, chose to shoot himself before they left.

American invasion

With this sorry episode at an end, things returned to the chaotic normalcy of regional warfare and brief presidential terms. One long-lived dictator, Ulises Heureaux (1882–99), was the exception to the rule, bringing a measure of stability by crushing his opponents more thoroughly than usual. But all such politicians raided the country's coffers, borrowed extravagantly from European governments, and sank the Dominican Republic further into insolvency. The threat of the country defaulting on its loans awakened foreign interest in its economic affairs, and gunboats were regularly dispatched by European powers to collect debts and, as a pretext, to protect their citizens.

The appearance of French or German gunboats in the Caribbean met with the strong disapproval of the United States, which since the mid-nineteenth century and the proclamation of the Monroe Doctrine in 1823 had viewed itself as the principal power in the Western hemisphere. Hostile to European power politics in the Americas, Washington was particularly alarmed that a bankrupt *caudillo* in the Dominican Republic might decide to sell or lease a part of the country to the Germans or British for a military base. Such fears deepened with the completion of the strategically essential Panama Canal in 1914 and growing suspicion of German aggression in Europe.

The permanent instability on the island of Hispaniola was thus a major cause of concern to Washington. Haiti was even more turbulent than the Dominican Republic, rocked by regular coups and civil conflict for a century since its independence. It was there that the Marines first landed in 1915, but the following year, after a particularly volatile period of political unrest, the US also occupied the Dominican Republic, sending troops into Santo Domingo in April 1916.

The main objective of the American occupation was to put the Republic's accounts in order and prevent other foreign powers from using its bankruptcy as a pretext for interference. A US Navy-run administration proceeded to run the country, organising tax collection and government spending. Some improvements took place; roads, schools and hospitals were built, and the endemic corruption of Dominican politicians was, temporarily at least, curtailed. But the Americans were also interested in expanding business opportunities for individuals and companies at home, and so began the wholesale Americanisation of the Dominican economy. The sugar industry, for instance, which had been run by a handful of Dominican magnates throughout the nineteenth century, was abruptly opened to US companies. With European beet sugar supplies cut off by the First World War, the price of Caribbean-produced sugar rocketed from 1915, and this coincided with a flood of US investment. American goods poured into the country, and the Dominican Republic briefly boomed on the back of foreign capital and high sugar prices.

There were winners and losers. The Dominican élite mostly did well out of joint ventures and access to US markets for their sugar. Quiet little towns such as La Romana and San Pedro de Macorís became bustling sugar-exporting centres, with grand new buildings and modern amenities. But the real victims were the Dominican small farmers and peasants, forced off their land by expanding plantations and new laws that abolished traditional forms of communal land ownership. As in Haiti, it was the rural

22

population that took up arms against the American occupying forces. Called *gavilleros*, these guerrilla bands harassed the US troops in outlying country districts and faced aerial bombings and concentration camps.

After nine years, the US withdrew, leaving a greatly changed country behind them. A modern sugar industry had been founded, antiquated land laws had been scrapped, and the rural poor were poorer than before. But perhaps most significant was the creation of a well-trained and well-armed *Guardia Nacional*, a military force intended to fight subversion and to limit the influence of regional *caudillos*.

The Chief

If the Americans thought they had ended the *caudillo* tradition in the Dominican Republic, they were to be severely disappointed. Rising rapidly through the ranks of the *Guardia Nacional* was one Rafael Leonidas Trujillo, an ex-cattle rustler and petty criminal who had all the attributes of the classic strongman. From a humble background, Trujillo was an ambitious character, joining the force in 1918 and becoming chief of the armed forces only a decade later. He was well placed to seize power in 1930 after a

▲ Rafael Leonidas Trujillo

feeble civilian government collapsed, and he ruled – either directly or through a series of puppet presidents – until 1961.

Trujillo was a megalomaniac of epic proportions. He encouraged a cult of personality and had himself titled The Benefactor, Excellency, *Generalísimo* and, more plainly, *El Jefe* (The Boss). Santo Domingo was renamed Ciudad Trujillo, flattering portraits hung everywhere, and schoolchildren studied The Benefactor's great deeds.

These, in truth, consisted mostly of theft and murder. He expropriated many of the country's assets, running the Republic like a family business, in which his equally brutal brothers and sons were co-directors. With huge interests in sugar, ranching, manufacturing and almost everything else, the Trujillo clan displaced many of the traditional élite families, thereby earning their hatred. By the time of his death, Trujillo was reputed to own three-quarters of the country's industries.

All opposition was crushed. Critics were jailed, exiled, or simply thrown to the sharks from deserted cliffs near Santo Domingo. Citizens could be arrested and 'disappeared' on the flimsiest of charges. Even those who lived abroad were not safe, as Trujillo's secret police snuffed out dissidents in New York and elsewhere. The US government disliked the dictator, but especially after Fidel Castro came to power in Cuba saw him as at least an ally against Communism. 'He may be a son of a bitch', said President Roosevelt, 'but he's *our* son of a bitch'.

▲ The car in which Trujillo was assassinated

For 30 years the dictator ruled, the jails filled with those who dared even to make jokes about him. He made no secret of his loathing for neighbouring Haiti, whose black population he despised, and in 1937 he ordered the massacre of some 10 000 Haitians who were working and living in the Dominican Republic. This massacre is remembered even today as the most appalling of his crimes.

The army and the Church officially supported Trujillo, but he had many enemies, not least among the country's old aristocratic families and those whose lives he had ruined. Eventually, in 1960, pressure began to mount, especially after a botched attempt by his henchmen to murder Venezuela's President Rómulo Betancourt. In May 1961 a group of military conspirators, allegedly helped by the CIA, shot The Benefactor dead as he drove to a romantic assignation.

Troubled times

After the three stifling decades of Trujillo's rule, his death unleashed a torrent of political activity and conflict. His family tried to cling onto power but were outmanoeuvred by the cunning Joaquín Balaguer, who had been puppet president at the time of the assassination. He, in turn, was edged out by the military, and a succession of short-lived administrations followed one another. Free elections were finally held in December 1962 and were overwhelmingly won by the Partido Revolucionario Dominicano (PRD), a moderate social-democratic organisation, led by Juan Bosch, a popular leader who had spent the preceding decades in exile.

▲ Juan Bosch with President John F Kennedy

But not everyone was pleased with the result. The Church distrusted Bosch's anti-clerical leanings, while the wealthy suspected him of Communist sympathies. His programme was, in fact, unambitious and his worst failing was his indecisiveness, but hostility grew against the PRD government, most crucially from the military. After only seven months, the army stepped in, with tacit US approval, and sent Bosch into exile.

With an unelected three-man *junta* running the country, Bosch's supporters, including some in the armed forces, organised resistance. A *coup* took place, with the aim of returning Bosch to the presidential palace, but almost at the same time a counter-*coup*, led by right-wing officers, erupted. Fighting broke out in the streets of Santo Domingo, and civil war loomed.

▲ US occupation (1965)

Again the Americans intervened, alarmed at the prospect of 'another Cuba'. Almost 25 000 US troops occupied Santo Domingo, keeping the warring factions apart and setting the foundations for new elections. Amidst great tension and rising anti-American feeling, the polling took place in June 1966, strictly supervised by American forces. A lacklustre Bosch was soundly defeated by the great survivor of Dominican politics, Joaquín Balaguer.

The Balaguer years

For six decades Dominican politics was dominated, openly or from behind the scenes, by Balaguer, an innocuous-looking but deeply ambitious student of Machiavellian power. First as Trujillo's puppet and then elected six times to the presidential palace, he mastered the science of Dominican politics, winning highly dubious elections and consolidating support among key sectors with lavish spending programmes.

After 1966 the PRD opposition was demoralised, and a paramilitary gang, known as La Banda, picked off high-profile activists. Seemingly unchallenged, Balaguer won elections in 1970 and 1974, presiding over a brief boom of high sugar prices and easy borrowing. But when, in 1978, he reluctantly allowed the PRD to take office after hotly disputed elections, the economy began to collapse. Huge debts, coupled with the global oil crisis, almost bankrupted the country, and the government was forced to accept the austerity measures prescribed by the International Monetary Fund (IMF). Riots and deaths ensued, as poor Dominicans, especially in the growing slums of Santo Domingo, felt the impact of government cuts and rising prices.

▲ Joaquín Balaguer

Balaguer was back in 1986 and clung to power until 1996, when finally yet another controversial election forced the US and others to suggest his retirement. Even then, the consummate operator was active, ordering his die-hard supporters to vote for the candidate of his choice. *Lo que diga Balaguer* (whatever Balaguer says) was their watchword.

In the meantime, the PRD had split into factions, and the breakaway Partido de la Liberación Dominicana (PRD), formed by the veteran Bosch, won elections in 1996. The charismatic young president, Leonel Fernández, marked a break with the Balaguer-Bosch years, but struggled to implement long-overdue economic reforms. He was replaced in 2000 by the PRD's Hípólito Mejía, a moderniser who promised further reforms and a better deal for the poor. Mejía, in turn, was voted out in May 2004 as Fernández returned for a second term.

Changing nation

In the years since Trujillo died, the Dominican Republic has made great strides in transforming its economy from one based almost entirely on sugar to a much more diversified mix of manufacturing, tourism and services. Sugar is still an important feature of the rural economy, and employs many thousands of Dominicans and low-paid Haitians from across the border, but compared to tourism and manufacturing it is almost obsolete.

▲ Cruise ship at anchor

Tourism is the big money-spinner nowadays, with more than two million visitors arriving from the US, Canada and Europe to stay in purpose-built resorts on the north and east coasts. Tourism earns the Republic at least $2 billion a year and creates countless jobs, from waiters to souvenir sellers. Manufacturing is also big business, worth some $3 billion annually, but much of this money is taken as profits by the foreign companies that employ low-wage workers to stitch T-shirts or jeans in special 'Free Trade Zones'.

The political landscape has also changed. Gone are the days of strongmen and military coups, and the Republic now enjoys a healthy democratic system, with clean elections and lively debate between three main parties. Dominicans are passionate about politics, and fresh election campaigns seem to start the day after polling, but there is little of the fear and violence associated with the past. In this sense, the Dominican Republic has finally found a sense of freedom that had eluded the country for half a century or more.

❷ From plantation to vacation

The Dominican Republic today

In half a century, the Dominican Republic has changed out of all recognition. Political freedom and a democratic system of government are now everyday realities, and the corrosive fear that was the principal feature of the Trujillo dictatorship has disappeared. The wholesale transformation of the country's economy from a sugar-dominated plantation system to a mixture of tourism and services has also altered people's lives. The Dominican Republic is no longer a rural, agricultural society, ruled by 'King Sugar', but rather an urban economy, where people are more likely to be employed in factories and hotels than in cane fields.

▲ New tourism complex

▲ Modern Santo Domingo

But this modernisation, while widespread, is by no means complete. Some areas of the Republic remain remote and attached to agricultural methods that have not changed for decades. There are parts of the country, especially near the Haitian border, that are still very poor, where jobs and government services are hard to come by. Throughout the Dominican Republic people still live in villages and small towns, which, despite the constant buzz of traffic, appear much the same as they did 50 years ago.

▲ Calle El Conde, Santo Domingo

▲ Urban style

▲ Guarding the presidential palace

Progress has certainly changed the face of the Dominican Republic, but not always evenly or fairly. The palatial homes of Santo Domingo's wealthy minority, with swimming pools, satellite dishes and armed guards, are a far cry from the crowded slums that surround the capital. Modern banks, corporate headquarters and hotels tell a story of financial growth, but abandoned sugar mills and poverty-stricken rural settlements suggest another economic reality.

This is also a country where the old and the new are intertwined. The Dominican Republic looks back to its Spanish roots and colonial traditions, but is also very much part of a modern, global network of communications and influences. Old-fashioned Hispanic courtesy exists alongside the imported youth

culture of the United States, centuries-old Creole recipes compete with fast food, colonial-style wooden buildings stand next to concrete office blocks. The high-rise business district of Santo Domingo is a different world from the dusty villages of the southwest.

Some of these contrasts and inequalities create conflict and social problems. Many Dominicans want to escape the poverty and boredom of the countryside for a brighter future in the city. Those already living in the shanty towns occasionally express their frustrations in riots and violence. But the interaction between the traditional and the modern, takes other, more positive, forms. Dominicans are often inventive and resourceful, and it is in their creative adaptation of old and new influences that the country's cultural energy takes shape.

A new economy

The Dominican Republic imports a good deal more than it exports, creating an ever widening trade gap. Its main imports are oil (mostly from Venezuela), food, cars and machinery and clothing parts – to be stitched into finished garments and re-exported. Its principal exports are ferro-nickel (mined by the Canadian-owned Falconbridge Company at Bonao), sugar, gold, coffee, tobacco and garments. The clothing is assembled in the Free Trade Zones and destined for the US market. In fact, the US accounts for over 80 per cent of the Dominican Republic's exports each year.

The gap between imports and exports (US$3–5 billion annually) is filled by income from tourism, worth $2 billion or more, and from other invisible exports. The country also receives at least $1 billion a year in hard currency from Dominicans living and working abroad. But even so, the Dominican Republic is heavily in debt, owing more than $5.5 billion to foreign governments and international lenders like the World Bank.

The government borrows from abroad partly to fund new developments like roads and ports, which it believes will help long-term development, but it also borrows to help pay off existing loans and to pay the huge number of Dominicans who work for the state. Political parties have always rewarded their voters by giving them jobs, and each incoming government tends to sack many existing employees and create new jobs for its own supporters. As a result, the payroll has grown enormously, taking up a large slice of the government's budget.

At the end of the 1990s it was estimated that 58.7 per cent of the workforce was employed by government and in other services, 24.3 per cent in industry and a mere 17 per cent in agriculture. This marks a huge shift from agriculture, which in the 1960s employed more than half the working population. Many people still work in the countryside, but the declining sugar industry, hit by low world prices, has cut its workforce and depends on cheap labour from Haitian immigrants.

▶ Chopping coconuts

Rich and poor

There are plenty of millionaires in the Dominican Republic. Some are descended from the old families that arrived in the early years of Spanish colonisation and own huge tracts of land. Much of this 'old money' tends to be based around the second largest city, Santiago de los Caballeros, the centre of cigar and rum manufacturing. There are also *nouveaux riches*, people who have done well out of tourism and other modern economic development. For all the wealthy life is sweet, with many servants, spacious homes and private education and health care in the US.

Many more Dominicans are poor, an estimated 25 per cent living below the poverty line in 2001. This means having to survive on

a couple of dollars a day or less. Naturally, existence for the poor is a struggle, and many are unable to afford medicines or school materials for their children. The slums of Santo Domingo show how people are forced to construct shacks from discarded wood and plastic, often without any sanitation or clean water.

◀ Riverside slum, Santo Domingo

▲ Shanty town children

Average annual income in 2001 was put at $5800: not a large sum with which to pay rent, buy food, and pay for schooling and health care. Yet most Dominicans manage on incomes at this level, sometimes by receiving regular cheques from relatives abroad, by doing extra work, or by growing their own food. All too often, though, families are unable to keep their children at school, for although primary and secondary education are free, children require books and other equipment and could, in any case, be earning money rather than going to school.

Women's work

Until the end of the Trujillo period, Dominican attitudes towards women were, to say the least, traditional. Women were expected to stay at home, look after children and do little else. Yet the fundamental changes in Dominican society over the last half century have also had a huge impact on women's roles and status. Nowadays, women make up a major part of the workforce, not just in tourism and commerce, but also in the Free Trade Zones, where they are preferred to men for their dexterity and reliability. They are also paid less than men, and trade union organisations have consistently accused some employers of exploitation.

Women are also conspicuous in the professions such as law and the media, while even in politics – traditionally the preserve of the *macho* strongman – individuals such as Milagros Ortiz-Bosch, vice-president from 2000 to 2004, have made their mark. As women begin to outnumber men in university education, this trend looks set to continue.

Yet women still face huge obstacles in Dominican society. Many are left as sole heads of households, as men abandon them or migrate in search of work. With little or no social security, single women with children struggle to balance work with family life. The Dominican media has also recently highlighted an alarming incidence of domestic violence directed against women by men.

Young nation

The 2002 national census revealed that out of a population of 8 230 772, some 40 per cent of Dominicans were under 18 years of age. This young population puts a strain on the country's limited educational resources and creates a number of social problems. A high proportion of children, for instance, fail to complete their education, preferring to look for work at the earliest possible opportunity. While child labour is illegal, the authorities can do little to stop children working with their parents in agriculture or informal-sector jobs.

▲ Street selling

◀ A school trip

A smaller number of children drift into crime and other anti-social behaviour. Begging and harassment of tourists used to be a problem in north coast resorts, but the government has managed to reduce this problem. Even so, there are considerable numbers of young Dominicans who earn a precarious living on the streets of Santo Domingo and other urban centres by cleaning shoes or selling goods.

As elsewhere, there is a considerable cultural clash between traditional values and modern fashions. Many young Dominicans, for instance, identify much more closely with the popular culture of the United States than with traditional Spanish-based habits and tastes. The proliferation of American influences through TV, the internet and films is gradually eroding time-honoured Dominican values of family life and respect for the Church. Most young people aspire to a North American lifestyle, and many indeed go in search of this dream by migrating to the US.

▲ Dominican beach chic

Figures of authority

The Trujillo dictatorship had two key pillars of support: the Catholic Church and the Dominican armed forces, although both would eventually abandon The Benefactor. In the years since, moreover, both have seen their influence wane, although throughout the 1960s and 1970s the military were active in politics.

The Church, of course, has a long history in the Dominican Republic, reaching back to the early years of the sixteenth century when priests spoke out against the mistreatment of the Taino population. But as time passed, the Church became increasingly identified with the rich minority and was itself a major landowner. Trujillo forced the Church hierarchy to collaborate with his regime, and although some priests bravely attacked his dictatorial methods, he managed to control the bishops and other senior figures.

As a result, the Church lost some of its moral prestige. Nowadays, some 90 per cent of Dominicans claim to be Catholics, but far fewer attend services regularly. Most Dominicans also prefer common law unions to Church-approved marriage.

The Catholic Church also faces spiritual competition from African-inspired religious beliefs, known collectively as *brujería*. Similar to but separate from Haitian *vodoun* (voodoo), *brujería* is thought to have its roots in religious practices imported by slaves. It combines appeal to Catholic saints with a belief in dark forces such as the 'evil eye', exerted by *brujos/as*, male and female priests. Few Dominicans will openly admit to practising *brujería*, but it is widely recognised that successful *brujos* have customers from all classes who

▲ Sentry duty in Santo Domingo

come in search of supernatural solutions to problems of love, money and family crisis.

The Dominican military has also seen its influence decline since the 1960s and is nowadays much less inclined to intervene in national politics. Most of the country's military manpower is involved in policing the border with Haiti, although there are frequent allegations that soldiers are involved in smuggling goods and people across the frontier.

Bad neighbours

The history of the Dominican Republic and Haiti is one of continual conflict and permanent hostility. Much of this animosity lies in two historical events: the Haitian occupation of the Republic (1822–44) and Trujillo's massacre of Haitians in the Dominican Republic (1937). But these events are part of a wider picture of distrust and dislike, which has roots in deep-seated issues of identity and race.

Although the great majority of Dominicans are of mixed race or black, with at least some African parentage, the country's official ideology stresses Dominicans' white, Spanish, Catholic heritage. In contrast, Haiti, where more than 95 per cent of people are black, is viewed from across the border as an African-descended nation, in which *vodoun* is more powerful than Catholicism. This view contains a good deal of racism and tends to project the 'civilised' Dominican Republic as superior to 'barbaric' Haiti.

Although a relatively poor country, the Dominican Republic is also much richer than its neighbour, the poorest in the Western hemisphere, where average income is only US$500 a year. As a result, Haitians have always come across the border in search of work and a better life. From the time of the American occupation they came to work on sugar plantations, doing arduous and badly-paid work that Dominicans refused to touch. The presence of Haitian migrant workers, some of whom have been in the country all their lives, has continued up to the present day.

▲ Haitian migrant

Nobody knows how many Haitians live and work in the Dominican Republic, with estimates ranging from 500 000 to a million. Many come and go across the 388-kilometre (241-mile) border, working seasonally, but there are also hundreds of thousands who live permanently in the Republic. Although their children have been born in the Dominican Republic, the authorities almost always refuse to grant them Dominican citizenship – which leaves them stateless. Human rights groups have also criticised conditions in the cane-cutters' encampments where many Haitians live. They have also condemned the occasional wide-scale deportations that take place whenever a Dominican government seeks to place the blame for any problem on the 'Haitian invasion'.

▲ Scraping a living

Haitians cut cane, but are also active in other agriculture, building and commerce. Haitian women are commonly employed by better-off Dominican families as maids. There is a bustling Haitian quarter in Santo Domingo, situated around the Mercado Modelo market, where Haitian paintings and handicrafts are visible. Along the border, at towns like Jimaní, Elias Piña and Dajabón, busy markets take place several days a week, with both Dominicans and Haitians buying and selling. In the border district, many people are bilingual in Spanish and Haitian Creole, and there is much business and contact across what is supposedly a heavily guarded frontier.

Dominican migration

▲ Dominican migrants, New York City

Just as Haitians come to the Dominican Republic to escape poverty, so many Dominicans choose to leave their homeland in search of a brighter future. The most popular destination is the United States, but there are also significant Dominican communities in Puerto Rico, Spain and other European countries.

All in all, there are believed to be over a million Dominicans in the US, of whom 750 000 are legal migrants. The others are undocumented, having overstayed a tourist visa or smuggled themselves in, normally via Puerto Rico. The centre of the Dominican community is New York City, where migrants live in areas such as Washington Heights. Dominican grocery stores, restaurants and music shops make these districts appear more Caribbean than American. There is a good deal of coming and going between the island and the US mainland, and many people send back regular payments to family at home.

Dominicans have made an enormous impact in baseball, with several top league players, and music, but are also associated with criminal activity. This is true only of a tiny minority of urban youths, but it has unfortunately affected popular perceptions of

Dominicans in the US. Gradually, however, as migrants and their children become more established and better educated, they are beginning to enter the professions and make a contribution to politics.

A smaller Dominican community in Puerto Rico is less conspicuous, as the US-run territory is Spanish-speaking and culturally similar. Some Dominicans brave the Mona Passage, the stretch of sea between the two islands, in overcrowded boats in a bid to reach Puerto Rico, from where illegal entry into the US is much easier. Others stay in Puerto Rico, which is much wealthier than the Republic, working in the informal sector or as domestic servants.

Transnational society

The existence of large Dominican communities overseas has turned the Republic into what sociologists have called a 'transnational society', a society that spreads beyond national borders. This has an effect on the nation's finances, as many millions of dollars are sent home each year and wealthy expatriates return with a small fortune to invest. On the negative side, it also means that many ambitious and intelligent people leave home to work abroad, depriving the country of some of its brightest hopes.

The advent of mass tourism has also contributed to the international flavour of the Dominican Republic, heightened further by the presence of large expatriate groups from the US, Canada and Europe. Drawn by the country's climate and culture, many foreigners come to set up businesses or to retire.

This mix of influences, together with the country's history of foreign occupation, is reflected in a diversity of ways. Santo Domingo, for instance, boasts restaurants of every conceivable national type: Spanish, Italian, French, even English, while any Dominican telephone directory reveals a truly international cocktail of names, from American and Italian to Middle Eastern and Eastern European.

In the course of the twentieth century, distinct communities came to settle in the Dominican Republic, often pushed by war or persecution in their homeland. Spaniards fleeing the Spanish Civil War arrived in the 1930s, as did almost a thousand Jewish refugees from Europe, who set up a colony in the north coast town of Sosúa.

They joined migrants who had arrived in the previous century, many from the Canary Islands and other parts of Spain, some from Italy, and a significant number from Palestine and Lebanon, who soon became heavily involved in trading and shopkeeping. The political history of the modern-day Republic contains many Arab-descended names: Majluta, Wessín y Wessín, Cury, Dipp.

Leaving aside ingrained hostility towards Haiti, this mixing of migrants and differing cultures has produced a mostly harmonious social blend. It is still the case that a white skin is preferable to a black one in terms of social mobility, but overt racism is rare in the Dominican Republic, for there are few people who are not descended from at least two ethnic backgrounds.

Cultural mixing and diverse influences explain much of the vitality of the Dominican Republic and its people. This is particularly the case in the field of art, literature and music.

❸ From merengue to mondongo
Music, food and the arts

Visitors' impressions of the Dominican Republic are often associated with noise, or particularly music. The unmistakably rhythmic pulse of merengue blares from shop doorways, from passing buses and taxis, while radios pump out high-decibel dance music in almost every street and bar. Music is part and parcel of the urban (and rural) scene; it is hard to avoid and, if you like Latin music, equally hard to resist.

Dominicans appreciate music of every variety. Orchestras and opera companies play to packed houses in Santo Domingo; international stars and bands perform at the mock-Roman amphitheatre at La Romana's Altos de Chavón complex; Dominican teenagers lap up the latest American trends on MTV. But the heart and soul of Dominican music – and arguably an intrinsic part of national identity – is merengue.

Merengue
Merengue's roots are thought to lie in a nineteenth-century fusion of European and African music. The rather staid European *contredanse*, meant for respectable couples, took on a local, but essentially African, rhythm. Bands of four musicians – playing the guitar-like *cuatro*, the double sided *tambora* or drum, the *marimba* and the rhythmically metal-scraping *güira* – produced the backing for vocalists who sang about social issues as well as engaging in risqué innuendo. The well-to-do looked down on this vulgar

▼ Dancing to merengue music

41

entertainment, but it grew in popularity, especially in the central Cibao region. Here, the accordion was the instrument of choice, especially in the oddly named *perico ripao* (literally 'ripped parrot') style of merengue, named after a Santiago brothel.

As foreign influences, not least the US occupation of 1916–24, added to the musical mix, bands expanded to include a brass section, piano, bass guitar and drum kit. The tempo remained fast, with the saxophones and trumpets adding a danceable syncopation. The lyrics, too, remained relevant to everyday concerns, the vocalists using a call-and-response structure to develop their themes.

Merengue might have remained a little-known local speciality were it not for the dictator Trujillo, who liked and sponsored the *merengue típico* of the Cibao. Looking for a 'national' sound and wanting to liven up tedious political meetings with something truly popular, Trujillo poured money into persuading bands to celebrate his achievements in song. As the music borrowed freely from jazz and swing, it adopted its characteristic big band sound.

Ironically, it was the repression of the Trujillo years that gave merengue its biggest boost, as The Benefactor disapproved of competition from abroad. When he was assassinated, a flood of US rock, soul and jazz as well as Cuban salsa entered the country, knocking merengue off its pedestal. But merengue had deep roots, and in the 1980s it staged an international comeback, pioneered by performers such as trumpeter Wilfrido Vargas and the flamboyant bandleader Johnny Ventura, who specialised in big band arrangements and elaborate choreography.

It was Juan Luis Guerra, however, who put Dominican music on the world stage with a string of best-selling albums in the 1990s. The US-trained composer and singer fused traditional merengue and other local genres with lush orchestration and sophisticated harmonics, producing classics such as *Bachata Rosa* and *Areito* that sold in millions. Guerra writes lyrics with great tenderness but also with a social edge, such as *Visa para un sueño*

▲ Juan Luis Guerra

(Visa for a Dream) about a desperate migrant's bid to cross the shark-infested Mona Passage to Puerto Rico.

Merengue is nowadays a transnational phenomenon, with many artistes based in the United States and playing to huge audiences there and across Latin America. Big money is involved, with some of this allegedly originating in the illegal drugs industry.

Bachata

If the Dominican Republic has become synonymous with merengue, it is also home to another, equally distinctive popular sound: *bachata*. Like merengue, this music has its origins in the country's lowlife, but this background of deprivation occurred later than that of merengue. Historians trace bachata's popularity to the 1960s when thousands of poor peasants, forced off their lands by hunger and the political clout of big landowners, crammed into the shanty towns of Santo Domingo. They brought with them a sort of country-and-western music, a melancholic mix of hard drinking and betrayed love, which thrived in the new urban context. Rather like Argentinian tango, this was the sound of the city's underclass, played in bars and brothels rather than glitzy venues.

As with merengue, it was Juan Luis Guerra who played a big part in spreading its popularity. Taking the maudlin feel of the music, he turned it into a romantic slow dance genre with sentimental lyrics and rich orchestral effects. Very different from the sprightly merengue, bachata mostly retained its languorous atmosphere. But over the years some bachata songs have taken on a quicker tempo, again enlivened by the syncopated brass section.

Modern music

Dominican popular music has always been open to external influences, from jazz and rock 'n' roll to Mexican mariachi and Latin American bolero. Neighbouring Haiti has had a significant musical impact, especially in the west of the country where the annual pre-Easter Rara street celebrations are boisterous affairs, while the Caribbean powerhouse of Cuba has also left its mark in the form of salsa and other styles.

Nowadays, the major imported flavours come from the United States, from where hip-hop and rap have reached the island via the large emigrant population of New York. These trends have been incorporated into the traditional folk genre of merengue, creating a dance hybrid called 'merenhouse'. Many merengue classics have been re-recorded in this style by bands such as Fulanito, who pay homage to their Dominican heritage by using accordion and traditional drums in high-tech remixes.

The latest artists and musical developments can be heard at innumerable retail outlets in all towns. Almost every hotel features live music or a disco, while the street corner *colmados* or grocery stores normally play the current hits as a background to beer drinking. But the real showcases are the two big annual merengue festivals, held on Santo Domingo's seafront *Malecón* in late July and early August and in the northern town of Puerto Plata in the first week of October. Sponsored by the nation's brewers and rum manufacturers, these crowded gatherings are loud and mostly good-natured.

Literature

The Dominican Republic was a late developer in terms of literature, especially when compared to the neighbouring territories of Haiti, Cuba and Puerto Rico. This is probably explained by its peculiar history of colonial neglect and foreign intervention, neither of which encouraged the conditions for literary self-expression. In fact, with few exceptions, it was only in the twentieth century that the Republic discovered its own authentic voice in literature.

The early colonial period was too poor and too violent to allow time for the creation or consumption of literature. The colonists were not literary, nor even literate, types, and no significant or lasting writing was produced by them or by their African slaves, whose cultural traditions mostly took the form of musical and oral storytelling. As for the indigenous Tainos, they left no permanent expressions of literary creation. The first writing came from outsiders: functionaries and priests. The military commander Gonzalo Fernández de Oviedo wrote a comprehensive history and assessment of the fledgling colony in the 1550s, while Bartolomé de Las Casas alerted the European public to the Taino genocide in his indignant *A Very Brief Account of the Destruction of the Indies* (1551).

As the Spanish colony slumbered its way through the sixteenth and seventeenth centuries, those few books that were read were imported from Europe. It was only after the 22 years of Haitian rule and the creation of the independent Dominican Republic that the first real examples of local writing materialised. These were mostly insipid and derivative works of poetry, heavily reliant on European Romanticism.

The first genuinely national novel appeared in 1882, and was a great success. Based on the exploits of the legendary Taino *cacique* or chieftain, Manuel de Jesús Galván's *Enriquillo* was a romanticised version of the colony's early history. It portrayed the Taino warrior as a 'noble savage' who eventually accepted

Christianity but who resisted foreign (i.e. Spanish) control. In the aftermath of Haitian occupation this struck a chord, as did the entirely mythical suggestion that modern Dominicans were descended from the heroic Tainos. For a people hard put to explain their dark colour but unwilling to admit to African ancestry (because that would make them no 'better' than Haitians), the idea of 'Indian' descent was most attractive. Even today, some Dominicans refer to their colour as 'Indio oscuro' (dark Indian).

The US occupation further encouraged a growing sense of national identity, but any literary Renaissance was crushed by the Trujillo dictatorship. The only literature that The Chief appreciated was the sycophantic praises churned out by government-paid hacks, and real writers were locked up, killed or exiled. Among these was Juan Bosch, later to become short-lived president, who wrote evocative short stories and elegant works of history in exile. His great rival, Joaquín Balaguer, was also a *littérateur*, producing poetry and historical fiction that was well received. From exile, the country's greatest poet, Pedro Mir, a political radical, wrote epic poems on the country's beauty and suffering.

There is
A country in the world
                          Located
On the very route of the sun
Hailing from the night.
                          Located
On a dreamlike archipelago
Of sugar and alcohol.

As with music, it is the transnational nature of Dominican society that has prompted interesting literary developments. The idea of being caught between Dominican and American influences has created a powerful hybrid literature, with Julia Alvarez and Junot Diaz the best-known exponents of modern cross-cultural writing. In books like *How the Garcia Girls Lost Their Accents*, Alvarez writes of the tensions of living in two different worlds, while Diaz's hard-hitting short stories, *Drown*, tell of gangland life and streetwise young Dominicans in New York.

Dominican art

In contrast to the vibrant and well-documented artistic creativity of neighbouring Haiti, the Dominican Republic has produced relatively little world-class painting or sculpture. Again, the impoverishment of the colonial period can be held responsible for a lack of artistic achievement, and it was not until the period following the Haitian occupation and the ejection of the Spanish in 1865 that Dominican painters began to produce work of lasting quality. These were mostly grandiose portraits of political dignitaries or wealthy individuals, or romanticised and idyllic landscapes.

Art was also very much the preserve of the social élite, with a painter such as Celeste Woss y Gil (1890–1985), daughter of a Dominican president, leading the way through much of the twentieth century. She set up an Academy of Painting and Drawing in 1930 and exhibited her oil paintings around the world. The 1930s also saw another important boost to Dominican art in the shape of several artists and intellectuals who had fled the Civil War in Spain. Among them was the left-wing José Vela Zanetti, whose father had been killed by Franco's Fascist thugs. Rather surprisingly, the Franco-admiring Trujillo took Zanetti under his wing and commissioned him to produce large murals for two of his private mansions as well as the great monument in Santiago.

▲ José Vela Zanetti

While Zanetti and others were producing social realism in the style of the great Mexican muralists, Jaime Colson (1901–75) established himself as the Republic's most accomplished artist. Born in Puerto Plata, Colson in fact spent little time in the Dominican Republic, preferring Barcelona, Madrid, Mexico City and Havana. His appreciation of Dominican themes, however, made him a leading exponent of a movement called *costumbrismo*, which sought to celebrate traditional Dominican rural life. Others more permanently based in the Republic benefited from the lifting of censorship after Trujillo's death, and from the 1970s onwards Dominican art began to reflect radical international trends. Much contemporary art is abstract and challenging, with brightly coloured tropical landscapes normally left to the itinerant vendors of Haitian 'naïve' paintings.

▲ Mass-produced Haitian art

There are many places in which the interested visitor can get a sense of the country's artistic life. Private galleries abound in the historical *zona colonial* of Santo Domingo. The capital's **Palacio de Bellas Artes** looks impressive from the outside, with its classical columns, but apart from the murals of Zanetti, exhibitions are rather sparse. Much more rewarding is the **Museo de Arte Moderno**, part of the modern cultural complex built by President Balaguer during the boom years of the 1970s. Here you can see the work of Jaime Colson and other examples of *costumbrismo*, evoking peasant life in the twentieth century. There are also more avant-garde paintings and sculptures on display, dramatising the Republic's mix of European, African and Latin American inspirations.

Sporting pastimes

Dominicans, males in particular, love sport. Athletes and sportsmen from the country have excelled over the years in running, boxing and polo. Santo Domingo offers good facilities for martial arts, tennis and horse racing, while almost every town of any size has its basketball court. One of the national obsessions is cockfighting, repellent to many visitors, but irresistible to large numbers of Dominican gamblers and enthusiasts. Sunday is usually the day for cockfighting, when pampered birds are proudly carried to the cockpit for an often short and lethal encounter with an opponent. Much rum is consumed and many pesos change hands in an unashamedly *macho* atmosphere. Once a purely rural activity with its roots in traditional Spanish culture, cockfighting now draws crowds from the urban middle classes in Santo Domingo's upmarket **Coliseo Gallístico**.

▲ Cockfighting

But the sport that really sets Dominican pulses racing is baseball, or *beisbol*. Football has almost no serious supporters in the Republic, but baseball is a countrywide religion, watched by everyone from children to grandmothers. Televisions and radios provide a constant diet of games, analysis and chat, while the newspapers often seem to carry more baseball than news stories.

This love affair with the American sport began early in the twentieth century, but on a strictly amateur basis and with few resources. The US occupation brought Dominicans into closer contact with baseball-playing Marines

▲ Baseball or *beisbol*

and encouraged an influx of US money and coaching skills into the national game. At first, it was concentrated around the big US-dominated sugar plantations, and even today it is the case that a high proportion of skilled players come from the poor sugar-workers' *bateys* around San Pedro de Macorís and La Romana. Predictably, in this politicised country, sport became mixed up with party rivalry, and the two main Santo Domingo teams, Licey and Escogido, sported the blue and red colours of the main political groupings.

As the sport evolved, talented Dominican players began to be recruited by bigger and wealthier clubs in Puerto Rico, Venezuela and Cuba, and then the US. At the same time, wealthy Dominican backers were able to attract mainly black players from the US to play in local teams. Inevitably, Trujillo took an interest in the sport, recognising its popular appeal, and one of his brothers ran a star-studded team in what was then Ciudad Trujillo, bankrolled by The Chief. But this expensive competition was ultimately unsustainable in a small and poor country, and the Golden Age of Dominican baseball fizzled out in the 1950s.

Thereafter the US major league teams set up almost permanent talent spotting facilities in the Dominican Republic, luring away eager young players with the promise of stardom and big money. Some have become household names in both the US and at home: Sammy Sosa, Pedro Martínez and Alex Rodríguez. Players of this calibre can expect to earn millions and become role models for hopeful youngsters across the country.

The national game, though deprived of its biggest stars, draws huge crowds from October to February. The main centres of the sport are the capital, Santiago and **San Pedro de Macorís**, where the baseball stadium dominates the town and the name of local prodigy Sammy Sosa is

◀ Baseball, La Romana

▲ Sammy Sosa, baseball star

revered. Clashes between rival teams are a raucous affair, with plenty of music, beer and snacks to accompany the action. Meanwhile, on almost every empty piece of wasteland in towns and villages alike, you will see young Dominicans swinging a bat at what is often a home-made ball.

Dominican food

Love of baseball is only matched by a love of good home cooking. Although the Dominican Republic received some adverse publicity a few years ago regarding food hygiene and upset tourist stomachs, this applied principally to buffet meals served in all-inclusive resorts and not to freshly prepared food available in restaurants and cafés throughout the country. Cheap Dominican food, it is true, tends towards the fried and greasy, but this is by no means inevitable.

What underpins most everyday meals is starch – in the form of rice, plantains, yams and other tubers. The counterpoint is spices and herbs: garlic, chilli, peppers and oregano, giving local food its distinctive kick. This national cuisine is normally known as *comida criolla*, and its most familiar dish is the so-called *bandera dominicana* (Dominican flag), a plate of stewed beef, rice, red beans, avocado and plantains, whose colours are meant to resemble the flag's. This staple dish is not usually spicy, but can be made so by the addition of pepper sauce.

Dominican food is essentially a blend of European and African ingredients. The foods that early Spanish colonists imported include chicken, beef, dairy products and, of course, sugar, while Taino staples were maize, cassava and fish. These have been mixed together, with other basics such as rice and bananas added, to produce the substantial mainstay of local cooking. Breakfast, for instance, may feature *mangú*, not mango but mashed plantain drizzled with oil and normally served with fried onions. Or try *sancocho*, a favourite across Latin America, a stew of at least five different meats and as many vegetables.

▶ North coast advertising

▲ Street food

Chicken is the commonest protein, and *arroz con pollo* (chicken and rice) is ubiquitous. But it is certainly worth trying goat (*chivo*), which can be served as a roast or a stew, both marinated and with plenty of herbs. A rib-sticking vegetarian alternative (although vegetarians are often offered little else but omelettes) is *mofongo*, another plantain-base delicacy. Be sure, however, not to confuse this with *mondongo*, an awesome tripe stew reputed to have anti-hangover properties.

Seafood and fish are specialities in every coastal resort, with fish often roasted (*al horno*), cooked with tomato and pepper sauce (*a la criolla*) or, best of all, grilled (*a la plancha*).

► Lobster on show

Fresh fruit is one of the great culinary pleasures, and there is normally an exotic fruit in season. Look out for *lechoza* (papaya), *chinola* (passion fruit) and *piña* (pineapple), all of which are grown locally. The abundance of fruit has led to the widespread availability of delicious *batidas*, milkshakes with real fruit pulp.

▲ Street selling

◀ Roadside fruit stall

Fast food

Burgers and KFC have made some inroads into the Dominican Republic, but most Dominicans sensibly prefer local versions of fast food. Street snacks such as *pastelitos* (turnovers stuffed with meat or cheese) are available almost everywhere in towns, as are the hot plantain chips called *platanitos*. Other favourites are the flat, meat-filled *empanadas* and *chicaronnes*, deep-fried portions of pork crackling. The Dominican version of fried chicken is found at roadside shacks advertising *pollo al carbón*. One step up is the low-budget *comedor*, a restaurant that will probably offer a limited menu but at rock-bottom prices. Although some places may look unprepossessing, the chances of an upset stomach are smaller than at the mass-produced hotel buffet. As a rule, it is better to order something that is cooked on the spot than food that has languished for some time under a heat lamp.

Drinking

Dominicans boast one of the highest per capita levels of alcohol consumption in the world, and beer and rum advertisements certainly feature prominently on billboards and the television.

▲ Brugal's modern rum factory

Wine is inevitably imported and relatively expensive, but beer, particularly the celebrated Presidente brand, is locally brewed and served ice cold. To appreciate Dominican beer it is worth going to a corner grocery or *colmado*, where a vast fridge will contain near-freezing bottles of Presidente and its rival Bohemia.

The country is a major rum producer, and three brands – Bermúdez, Brugal and Barceló – dominate. There are light and dark rums, some of the latter being specially aged (they are called *añejo*) for a more mellow flavour. Rums are mixed with Coke, other soft drinks or fruit juices, but the best are drunk simply with ice or like a good brandy.

Tea is almost unknown, and coffee can be disappointingly bland when served in hotels. The best coffee is to be had in local bars, freshly made and extremely cheap.

A Dominican night out

Dominicans tend to be sociable, and weekends and public holidays are always an excuse for a good night out. A warm climate encourages outdoor gatherings, and it is common, as in Spain, to see families taking a leisurely stroll around the nearest *plaza*, park or seafront boulevard (after the daily dose of televised soap operas). Families and groups of friends also like to sit out at night in quiet back streets or on balconies, chatting and watching passers-by.

For the less staid, the main social activities are drinking and dancing. Most towns have at least two or three discos, some offering high-tech lighting and a sophisticated sound system. Others are more down-to-earth, but the atmosphere is usually friendly and the mix of salsa, merengue and bachata very loud. Most hotels offer some night-time entertainment. The dress code is normally casual but smart. Shorts are definitely not worn to anything other than beachside bars.

The accepted drinking etiquette for a group is to order a bottle of rum, a bucket of ice and a handful of soft drinks. This works out cheaper then buying individual drinks and is a good way of mixing with the locals.

Dominicans start their night out late and end it even later. Noise can be a problem in popular resorts and on busy streets such as Santo Domingo's *Malecón*, as cars pump out high-octane music until dawn. A double-glazed hotel room is a must.

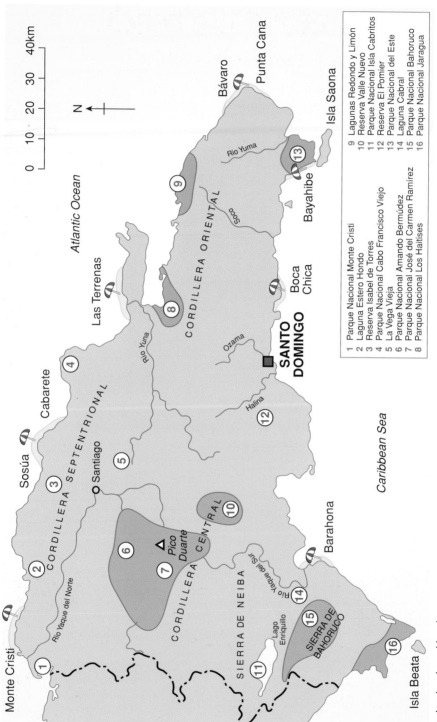

National parks and beaches

Atlantic Ocean

Caribbean Sea

N

| 0 | 10 | 20 | 30 | 40km |

Monte Cristi
Sosúa
Cabarete
Las Terrenas
Bávaro
Punta Cana
Isla Saona
Bayahibe
Boca Chica
SANTO DOMINGO
Santiago
Barahona
Isla Beata

CORDILLERA SEPTENTRIONAL
CORDILLERA ORIENTAL
CORDILLERA CENTRAL
SIERRA DE NEIBA
SIERRA DE BAHORUCO

Pico Duarte

Río Yaque del Norte
Río Yaque del Sur
Río Yuma
Río Yuma
Soco
Ozama
Halina
Lago Enriquillo

1 Parque Nacional Monte Cristi
2 Laguna Estero Hondo
3 Reserva Isabel de Torres
4 Parque Nacional Cabo Francisco Viejo
5 La Vega Vieja
6 Parque Nacional Amando Bermúdez
7 Parque Nacional José del Carmen Ramírez
8 Parque Nacional Los Haitises
9 Lagunas Redondo y Limón
10 Reserva Valle Nuevo
11 Parque Nacional Isla Cabritos
12 Reserva El Pomier
13 Parque Nacional del Este
14 Laguna Cabral
15 Parque Nacional Bahoruco
16 Parque Nacional Jaragua

➍ Beyond the beach
Nature and outdoor activities

Many visitors to the Dominican Republic assume that the country's natural beauties are mostly confined to its beaches. While it is true that there are magnificent expanses of sand suited to every taste and activity, this is by no means the whole story when it comes to natural attractions. Instead, the Dominican Republic offers an extraordinary array of landscapes and outdoor pursuits, ranging from mountain hiking and cycling to windsurfing and whale-watching. Its flora and fauna are much more varied than in most other Caribbean islands, as are its natural habitats, covering the spectrum from tropical forest to cactus-studded desert.

▲ South coast beach

A series of mountain ranges give the country its varied and often dramatic terrain. The biggest is the **Cordillera Central**, stretching eastwards from the Haitian border to turn southwards

▼ Pico Duarte – the highest mountain in the Dominican Republic

▲ Cordillera Central landscape

and end near the Caribbean coast. The highest point is the **Pico Duarte** (3175 metres/10 425 feet), whose summit is often hidden in clouds. The range's lower mountains, and the sheltered valleys between them, are home not just to forests and fast-moving rivers but to some of the country's most productive farmland. Another range runs parallel to the Atlantic north coast, separating the second city of Santiago from the sea. This line of mountains, the **Cordillera Septentrional**, is smaller than its central equivalent, reaching 1240 metres (4071 feet), but providing a dramatic backcloth to the north coast resorts.

Other ranges provide rugged landscapes in the southwest and east. The hundred-kilometre (62-mile) long **Sierra de Neiba**, which marks the border with Haiti, rises to 2279 metres (7483 feet), while to the south, the **Sierra de Bahoruco** reaches 1931 metres (6340 feet) in a remote chain of forest-covered peaks. To the east, the **Cordillera Oriental** is more a line of rolling green hills than a mountain range as such.

Despite being a relatively poor country, with significant pressures on natural resources, the Dominican Republic has succeeded in protecting a good deal of its natural environment. In contrast to neighbouring Haiti, where overpopulation and poverty have resulted in the ecological disaster of wide-scale deforestation, the Republic boasts large tracts of forest and mangrove. At the heart of this environmental success story is the network of national parks.

National parks

There are some 70 protected areas within the Dominican Republic, administered by the state-run Dirección Nacional de Parques (DNP). They cover a wide range of natural sites: mountains, forests, estuaries, rivers and mangroves. Others are intended to safeguard places of special archaeological or historic importance. Some are small sites of scientific interest, others are extensive tracts of woodland or dry forest, protected because of their particular flora and fauna. Visitors may enter some of these areas, where there are facilities and guides; others are off limits. The main DNP office is to be found in Santo Domingo, where permits can be obtained to visit national parks. The parks themselves also have administrative offices where permits can be bought.

The biggest and perhaps most spectacular territories under DNP protection are the two adjoining parks in the Cordillera Central. Both have been protected areas since the 1950s, hence reducing the impact of settlement and deforestation. The more northerly **Amando Bermúdez National Park** covers 766 square kilometres (295 square miles) of mountainous subtropical rainforest in the foothills of the Pico

▶ Amando Bermúdez National Park

Duarte. Here are vast forests of native pines, and the temperature is surprisingly low. In the months of December and January, for instance, temperatures of -8°C have been recorded, cold enough for a frost. Hikes can be organised through the DNP office in the village of **La Ciénaga**, from where it is possible to make an ascent of the Pico Duarte.

To the south lies the **José del Carmen Ramírez National Park** (764 square kilometres/295 square miles), again home to tracts of pine and other conifers. It is here that several rivers have their sources, not least the Río Yaque del Sur, which runs down the mountains to provide irrigation and hydro-electricity in the plains below. To the east is the 657 square-kilometre (254 square-mile) **Valle Nuevo National Park**, not far from the beautiful Constanza Valley, a prosperous farming area with an alpine landscape. The park itself is cool and sheltered, with many streams and a profusion of bird life.

In complete contrast to these temperate and pine-clad mountain wildernesses are the coastal eco-systems within the DNP administration. The biggest of these is the **Los Haitises National Park** (200 square kilometres/77 square miles) on the south coast of Samaná Bay. This is a weird landscape of small, bumpy hills, known as *mogotes*, some of which rise out of the sea. With extensive mangroves and caves, some containing images scratched on the walls by Tainos many centuries ago, the isolated region is a magnet for eco-tourists. Whatever negative impact they might have, however, is limited by the fact that there are no roads in the park (all visits to the karst caves and their stalactites take place in boats).

◀ Boats at Bayahibe

▲ Parque Nacional del Este

On the south coast near Bayahibe and Boca de Yuma, the 430 square-kilometre (166 square-mile) **Parque Nacional del Este** was established in 1975 and is a paradise for many indigenous bird species. A peninsula comprising dry and subtropical forest, caves and unspoilt beaches, the park also includes the **Isla Saona**, a small island whose palm-lined beaches are reminiscent of the most idyllic travel agent's brochure. Scarcely inhabited but for a couple of fishing communities, the Isla Saona does attract large crowds of tourists, but it is still possible to find a quiet stretch of beach. The park also has a network of caves, including the **Cueva José María** with over 1000 Taino images on its walls. In 1997 a team of archaeologists discovered a further Taino cave system in a remote part of the inland park, complete with extensive remains. It is believed that this was the site of a Spanish massacre of Tainos in 1503.

▲ Taino petroglyphs in Cueva José Maria

59

Dotted around the country, the other national parks include the dry and hostile **Monte Cristi National Park** on the north coast by the Haitian border, where pelicans, egrets and frigate birds thrive in lagoons, and the extensive **Sierra de Bahoruco National Park** near Barahona in the southwest. Here the protected territory rises steeply from the coast to reach more than 2500 metres (8208 feet), providing a home for no fewer than 166 species of orchid. Further down the coast towards Oviedo, the **Jaragua National Park** is the largest in the country, encompassing the wild and uninhabited islands of Beata and Alto Velo. Here are to be found 60 per cent of the country's bird species, which find sanctuary in the unwelcoming landscape of cactus, scrub and rocky outcrops. This undeveloped corner of the Republic is extremely hot and dry, but inside the park is the **Laguna de Oviedo**, a vast saltwater lake that attracts flocks of flamingos.

Perhaps the most unusual of these natural sites is also in the southwest, only an hour's drive from Barahona. The **Isla Cabritos National Park** is comprised mostly of a bone-dry limestone and coral island sitting in the salty water of the Lago Enriquillo. This unpromising-looking island, measuring 12 kilometres (7 miles) in length, is home not just to turtles and large iguanas, but also to crocodiles. A short boat trip from the DNP office takes the visitor to this hot and rocky place, where disconcertingly tame iguanas come to inspect the tourists.

Flora and fauna

Despite five centuries of agriculture, mining and, most recently, tourism, the Dominican Republic has retained a wide array of animal and plant life. Colonisation meant the importation of foreign species such as horses, dogs and rats, while the landscape has been irreversibly altered by the arrival of sugarcane, bananas and other imported crops. But despite the steady spread of human habitation and activity, the Republic's mountainous geography and varied climate has ensured that many species of plant and animal have survived and even prospered.

Apart from imported animals, there are few mammals. The hutia, a small, shy rodent, is nocturnal, living in caves or in tree hollows. It is threatened, as is the solenodon, a larger rat-like and long-nosed animal that eats insects. An altogether bigger mammal is the manatee or sea cow, a distant relative of the elephant. These gentle vegetarian creatures live in the wilder mangrove areas around the coast, feeding on organic matter. They can weigh more than 1000 kilos when fully grown, taking on a rounded shape with two small flippers. Much more common are several species of bat, to be seen in the many caves in the national parks.

▲ Manatee

If the mammals are disappointing, the reptiles and amphibians are certainly not. The American crocodile, for instance, can reach 4 metres (13 feet) in length and can be seen in considerable numbers in and around Lago Enriquillo and the Monte Cristi area. They often share their habitat with the large rhinoceros and Ricord iguanas, the former growing up to 2 metres (6 feet). Both are herbivorous and shy, although those in the Isla

▲ Iguana

Cabritos National Park are distinctly curious about humans. Lizards of various sizes and colours are to be found almost everywhere, from stony deserts to suburban gardens. Four species of turtle are indigenous to the Dominican seas; the leatherback is more common than the hawksbill, but all are under threat from illegal hunters in search of turtle meat and valuable shells.

Marine life in general has come under sustained attack from people, and much of the coral reef that once surrounded the country is now gone, destroyed by pollution and destructive fishing. One of the few exceptions is the **Banco de la Plata** (Silver Banks) **Scientific Reserve**, some 140 kilometres (87 miles) out to sea north of Puerto Plata. Here the government has established a reserve, where coral reefs and turtles are protected. Most spectacular, however, is the arrival every year between December and March of thousands of breeding humpback whales. Thousands arrive every day in this mating ground, often rising majestically out of the water and hurling themselves down with a great splash. Day trips from Puerto Plata can be arranged, while the seas around Samaná Bay, also accessible by boat, contain pilot whales and dolphin.

Insect life, sometimes unfortunately, is plentiful, although the Dominican Republic does have some large and beautiful butterfly species, especially in the dry southwest. Altogether less welcome are the ubiquitous mosquitoes, whose bite carries the risk of dengue fever, and scorpions. Snakes there are, but they are non-venomous.

There are some 300 species of bird in the Republic all year round, with a further 200 from colder climates over wintering. Again, the wild southwest is the best place for birdwatching, especially in the salty lakes and lagoons. These places are favoured by flamingos, herons and egrets, while the freshwater lakes attract ducks and grebes. The dense mangroves that are still to be found in more inaccessible areas provide shelter to brown pelicans, frigate birds and cormorants.

 Humpback whale

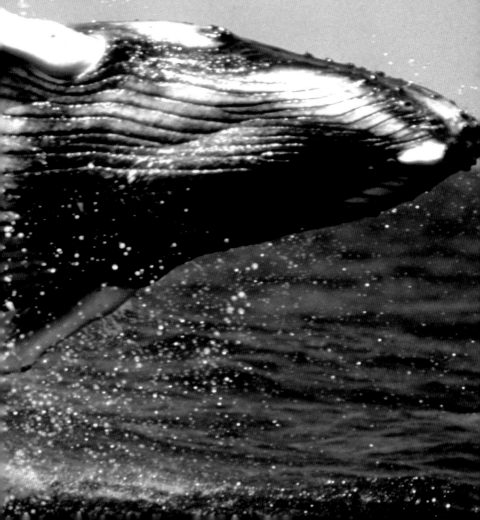

The mountainous terrain of the Cordillera Central is another suitable habitat for a wide range of birds, several of them named after the island itself. Among the pine forests live the endangered Hispaniolan parakeet, mostly green but with flashes of red, and the Hispaniolan woodpecker. More easily spotted is the Hispaniolan emerald hummingbird, which shares its eye-catching colour with the Hispaniolan parrot, a bright green and very chatty bird. Not all birds are green, however; one of the commonest species is the white cattle egret, to be seen in fields throughout the country, and the brown palm chat or *Cigua palmera*, a thrush-like bird that nests high in the crown of a palm tree, is the national bird.

Palm trees are a feature of the Dominican Republic, with the country boasting some 60 varieties. The tallest and most graceful is the indigenous royal palm, reaching 20 metres (66 feet) in height. Not only are its nuts edible, but its leaves have traditionally been used in rural districts for thatched roofs. The more common coconut palm is much in evidence, as is the so-called hat palm, with its fuzzy clumps of foliage. Many palms are to be found along beaches, often joined by sea grape and in more remote areas, different forms of mangroves.

One of the first commodities to be exported by the Spanish was the valuable local mahogany, which has become rare as a result of logging. It remains the national plant. Other more common tree species are the West Indian cedar and the Creole pine, the latter covering much of the Cordillera Central. Mountain trees also include myrtle, cherry and juniper, while in the hot plains there are acacias, frangipanis and poisonwood. The arid districts in the west are filled with cacti of all shapes and sizes, and the prickly pear is much in evidence.

The full array of the country's flowers can be appreciated in Santo Domingo's **Botanic Gardens**, which contain 300 species of orchid as well as bromeliads and water lilies. The Dominican Republic is now a major exporter of plants and flowers into the North American market, and some farmers in the fertile Constanza region grow roses and lilies especially for export. Otherwise, the country is colourful with bougainvillea and hortensias, flamboyants and heliconias.

Even in this natural paradise there are plants that should be avoided. Most common is the *pringamosa,* a low-growing shrub with leaves like those of a marrow or pumpkin plant. When touched, these produce an agonising mix of pain and itchiness. It is always worth remembering, too, that falling coconuts can be lethal.

▲ The Botanic Gardens

▼ Bougainvillea

▲ Horse riding

Hiking, cycling and riding

The relative coolness of the mountain areas makes energetic walking and off-road cycling possible. The most popular hiking trails are to be found in the national parks within the Cordillera Central. It is possible to make the demanding ascent of the **Pico Duarte**, which can take up to six days, but it is obligatory to hire an official guide. The easiest way to arrange this very strenuous hike is to start from the DNP office in the village of **La Ciénaga**. It should be remembered that hikers have to sleep in very rudimentary cabins and face cold night-time temperatures. But the views from the peak of Duarte, where no trees grow, are spectacular, reaching on a clear day to Lago Enriquillo and the Caribbean Sea. An even longer hike starts at the **Presa de Sabaneta** dam, north of San Juan de la Maguana. Comprising around 100 kilometres (62 miles) of remote countryside, this is for the energetic only.

Less gruelling hikes can be undertaken both in the Cordillera Central and elsewhere in the country. The cool uplands around **Jarabacoa** and **Constanza** are a mix of pine forests and farmland, with many villages and settlements dotted around the alpine scenery. In the southwest it is feasible to drive some way up into the **Sierra de Bahoruco** and walk through empty expanses of pine forest. A less ambitious but rewarding hike can be found in the north coast town of Puerto Plata, where a four-hour trek takes the walker to the top of **Mount Isabel de Torres**, the 800-metre (2627 feet) high mountain that looks over town and sea. Horses can also be hired, or the least demanding method of reaching the top is to take the cable car. Even here it is advisable to hire the services of a guide.

Cycling has become popular in recent years, especially with the advent of robust mountain bikes that can cope with rough tracks. Even so, there are only a handful of tour operators that rent out bikes of good quality. As with hiking, the preferred cycling area is within the Cordillera Central, especially around Constanza and Jarabacoa. The road between these two towns is too rough for most vehicles, but it is manageable on a good mountain bike. The advantage of this sort of travel is that stopping and meeting people en route is extremely easy.

The same is true of horse riding, and here the Dominican Republic offers more choice than with cycling. Some riding is strictly amateur, lasting no more than an hour or so, but there are also more serious excursions on offer, especially from **Rancho Baiguate** near Jarabacoa. Dominican horses tend to be on the small side, but are sturdy and used to rough mountain tracks. There are also horse riding facilities near Cabarete on the north coast, in the east near Hato Mayor and Higüey (**Rancho Jonathan**). Hotels in Punta Cana and Bávaro can arrange excursions here, and there is also a *rancho* in Punta Cana itself, from where you can ride along large expanses of beach.

Adventure activities

Most inland water sports are based around Jarabacoa, where **Rancho Baiguate** organises a number of activities in the region's fast-moving rivers. These include rafting down the **Río Yaque del Norte** in a rubber boat (guided by an experienced instructor), where a group of rafters armed with paddles avoid rocks and descend white water rapids. Alternatively you can attempt canyoning, jumping into a river gorge while suspended by a rope and harness. Cascading takes place at waterfalls, where the

▼ Whitewater rafting

hardy climber abseils through the cascade before leaping into the pool at the bottom. More conventional is kayaking, also practised on the Río Yaque del Norte under the aegis of **Aventuras del Caribe**. With all these sports the best time of year is between November and May, as the rainy season guarantees faster-flowing water.

There are caves situated throughout the country, many with Taino petroglyphs clearly visible on the walls. Some offer easy access, but others require greater planning and equipment. The caves within the **Parque Nacional del Este** can be visited with a DNP-approved guide, revealing stalagmites, stalactites and masses of bats as well as indigenous art. A similar experience is on offer at the **Los Haitises National Park**, where several large grottoes contain Taino images and are reputed to have been the hideout of pirates such as 'Calico Jack' Rackham.

Beaches and water sports

The Dominican Republic can lay claim to some of the finest beaches in the world. These include busy resort beaches, wild Atlantic-facing stretches of sand and the long, reef-sheltered shores of the eastern tip. Each coastline, whether Atlantic or Caribbean, has its own characteristics, while resorts differ considerably in atmosphere and amenities. There is also considerable variety in terms of water sports, ranging from world-class windsurfing in north coast **Cabarete** to placid beach games in the tourist towns on the south coast.

▼ Crowded Cabarete

The north coast offers the excitement of Atlantic surf as well as miles of pristine white sand. Cabarete has become an international windsurfing mecca since the 1980s and now caters almost exclusively to surf aficionados. Its reputation for water sports has also encouraged providers of other activities to set up shop, offering rides of every description and sometimes drawing big crowds. Yet only a few miles west around a headland are the more relaxed and traditional seaside resorts of **Playa Dorada** and **Sosúa**, where sunbathers lie in serried rows and souvenir vendors ply their trade. On the so-called **Silver Coast** hectic resorts alternate with quiet beaches. To the west of Puerto Plata the beaches around **Luperón** are often almost empty, as is the magnificent **Playa Grande** near Río San Juan to the west. Further west, the **Samaná Peninsula** juts out into the Atlantic, offering access to Atlantic and Caribbean alike. **Cayo Levantado**, the paradise island used in 1970's Bacardi commercials, can be reached by ferry from the town of Samaná, while to the north of the peninsula is **Las Terrenas**, once a quiet fishing village and now a centre for European expatriates. It has some of the country's best beaches, lined by palm trees and fringed with perfect white sand.

The south coast, especially near Santo Domingo, has beach resorts that are busy and noisy, especially at weekends. **Boca Chica** and **Juan Dolio**, in particular, are popular with weekenders from Santo Domingo and have a somewhat tawdry feel. But further east, beyond La Romana, the crowds thin out, and places like Bayahibe retain something of the atmosphere of an old-fashioned fishing village, even though big tourist installations are close by. Here there are plenty of water sports on offer, including diving and excursions to the nearby national park. Even more off the beaten track, however, are the wild beaches that line the Caribbean coast southwest of Barahona. Villages like **Paraíso** and **Los Patos** are fronted by miles of undeveloped sand, where you are as likely to see goats as tourists roaming the beach. Snorkelling and diving are recommended in the **Bahía de Neiba** near Barahona, where manatees can be spotted.

The eastern tip of the Republic houses the most recently constructed tourist complexes, which owe their existence to the vast stretches of beach that line the coast. Unfortunately, much of the 30 kilometres (19 miles) of beach in **Punta Cana** and **Bávaro** is cordoned off by the large hotels, blocking access to locals and other non-residents. One exception is the beachside community of **Cortecito**, where restaurants and water sports are open to all. The idyllic beaches spread northwards far beyond the tourist enclaves, but access to them is tricky as roads are few and primitive. At **Playa Limón** near the entrance to the Bahía de Samaná there are unspoilt mangroves and deserted vistas of sand, although the current is reputedly dangerous.

▲ Samaná Beach

Most beaches are safe unless hotels or other locals say otherwise, and children normally face few risks apart from sand fleas and sunburn. Even more painful, however, is the sting delivered by sea urchins. A different problem in some popular resorts are the over-persistent vendors and hawkers whose presence often causes annoyance. This problem is kept to a minimum in the exclusive beach properties of big hotels or by going to more remote spots.

Common water sports like snorkelling and diving are almost ubiquitous except in the most inaccessible areas. Diving is particularly good around **Sosúa** and **Monte Cristi** on the north coast, while in the southeast the recommended spot is **Bayahibe**, from where the national park and the Isla Saona can be reached. Of particular interest to divers is the **Isla Catalina**, offshore from La Romana, which has the best coral reef on the south coast.

For the less energetic, a trip to the **Acuario Nacional** (National Aquarium) on Santo Domingo's coastal **Avenida España** offers an insight into the diverse inhabitants of the sea. Large tanks contain sharks, moray eels and manta rays, a sight likely to deter all but the most courageous from venturing too far into the water. More appealing is Tamaury, the orphaned manatee, reportedly rescued from near Barahona when its mother was killed.

⑤ Santo Domingo
Cradle of the Americas

First impressions of the Dominican Republic's capital are not always positive. The road from the Las Américas airport to the east runs along the coast, with waves crashing over rocks and lines of stately palm trees. But soon the open views give way to ramshackle development: shacks and breeze-block structures, abandoned cars and small factories. As the city approaches, low-level concrete apartments and rickety wooden houses draw closer together, interspersed with little corner stores and workshops. People are everywhere, the traffic becomes dense, the noise of music, *motoconchos* (motorbikes) and human activity mounts.

▲ Colonial style

But suddenly your taxi passes the great gaunt outline of the Columbus Lighthouse, crosses the slow-moving Ozama River and turns left down congested shopping streets to arrive in what is one of the most beautifully preserved colonial towns in the Americas. Surrounding buildings are no longer of concrete or cinder-block but centuries-old stone. Some are 500 years old. Elegant plazas, cobbled streets and traditional lanterns give the sense of a bygone age. This is the *zona colonial*, the historic heart of Santo Domingo and the site of the first permanent European settlement in the Western hemisphere.

The zona colonial

Although a small part of the sprawling city, the *zona colonial* is its architectural showcase, containing in no more than a couple of square kilometres some of the finest examples of early Spanish colonial building anywhere in the world. The district stretches up about 12 blocks from the Ozama, criss-crossed by streets that form the classic New World colonial grid system. Within this tight-knit and low-level *barrio* (there are few modern buildings and no high-rise structures) are fortresses, churches, religious communities, grand palaces and more modest homes, embellished by spacious plazas, parks and waterside views. Not that all intruding signs of modernity have been avoided; an ugly power station and a concrete silo are all too visible on the banks of the Ozama, while the main commercial thoroughfare, the **Calle Conde**, owes more to twentieth-century functionalism than colonial heritage. But even so, the *zona colonial* remains a beautifully restored and protected jewel. Its renovation began in the 1970s after centuries of neglect, but it was the five hundredth anniversary of Columbus' arrival, celebrated in 1992,

Zona colonial face

that accelerated the reconstruction and cleaning up of the area as the government sought to show off the city's colonial delights to the outside world.

Governor Ovando, Plaza España

The city's beginnings in 1496, after the abortive first settlement on the north coast, were unpromising. An initial attempt to found a city on the east bank of the Ozama was reputedly foiled by a plague of ferocious ants. The Spanish colonists then moved across the river and put down foundations on the present site. The first priority was defence, from hostile Tainos or marauding pirates, and the **Fortaleza Ozama** dates from 1503, built by Governor Nicolás de Ovando. Ovando's grand residence is slightly to the north, renovated and transformed into a luxurious hotel. The walls of the fortress have been repaired many times since

Fortaleza Ozama

their first construction, not least after Sir Francis Drake demolished much of the city in 1586, but much of the original stone is still in place. The calm open space within the walls is overshadowed by the **Torre del Homanaje** (Homage Tower), a watchtower that was later used as a prison and is now a small museum. Views of the colonial district and river activity can be enjoyed from the top of the tower. Attached to the fortress is the **Casa de Bastidas**, a grand sixteenth-century residence that belonged to Rodrigo de Bastidas, the royal tax collector who went on to found the coastal city of Santa Marta in Colombia. Another colonial trailblazer lived across the street from Bastidas; Hernán Cortés, the *conquistador* of Mexico, lived at the **Casa de Francia** before setting off on his expedition in 1519. His home is thought to date from 1503, and today this imposingly arcaded building is occupied by the French Embassy.

All these early colonial edifices, built from weathered coral stone, line the first of the capital's streets, the **Calle Las Damas**. This cobbled thoroughfare, running parallel to the river, was named after the elegant Spanish ladies who used to stroll along it in the cool of the evening. Nowadays most of what were originally mansions, built to reflect the power and prestige of the early colonists, are museums, shops or galleries. One exception is the later **Panteón Nacional** (National Pantheon), built in the early eighteenth century as a Jesuit convent. When the Jesuits were expelled by the Spanish in 1767, this austere classical building passed through various hands, suffering the indignity of being used as a tobacco warehouse and theatre.

▲ Calle Las Damas

▲ National Pantheon

▼ Las Casas Reales

It was the dictator Trujillo who had the building restored in the 1950s as a suitable resting place for various national heroes, and it was here that he intended himself to be buried. His ambition was to be thwarted, however, and he was eventually interred in Paris after his assassination in 1961. Marble caskets containing the remains of Dominican luminaries such as the veteran *caudillo* Pedro Santana surround an eternal flame. Marble floors, a vast copper chandelier donated by Trujillo's fellow dictator General Franco, and ornate ceiling murals, contribute to an atmosphere of solemnity, watched over by a uniformed sentry.

Another intriguing glimpse into Dominican history is to be had a few doors further along the street at the **Museo de Las Casas Reales**. This reconstructed sixteenth-century building (in fact, two adjoining mansions) was where the *Real Audiencia*, the judicial and administrative council for the colony sat. So that these grandees would know the time, a sundial, the **Reloj del Sol**, was positioned across the road to catch most of the day's sunshine. Nowadays the museum holds a rather disorganised collection of historic objects, including Taino relics, old coins and artefacts from the colonial period. The most interesting items are those salvaged from various shipwrecks.

The Calle Las Damas ends in the large and seemingly empty **Plaza España**, closed to traffic and guarded by a statue of Governor Ovando. On the north side stands a group of sixteenth-century buildings known as **Las Atarazanas**, once a row of warehouses and an arsenal, now restored to house cafés and tourist shops. A museum at one end of this whitewashed terrace contains more treasure recovered from shipwrecks.

▽ Las Atarazanas

▲ Alcázar de Colón

Opposite is perhaps the most striking building in the *zona colonial*, a two-storey coral-stone palace, with ten elegant arches and two flanking palm trees. This is the **Alcázar de Colón**, built by Christopher Columbus' son Diego when he succeeded Ovando as governor in 1509. Not a single nail was used in the construction of this imposing symbol of authority, its thick stone walls serving as a fortification against uprisings. Diego lived here with his aristocratic Spanish wife, María de Toledo, and it was to all intents and purposes the headquarters of the Spanish Crown in the early days of the colony. It fell into disrepair after Drake's ransacking in 1586, and in 1770 the building was abandoned, slowly crumbling away until 1957 when craftsmen began to restore its façade and damaged arches. Today it contains a museum with furniture and artefacts from Diego's period, while the exterior is one of the finest examples of the Moorish-influenced Gothic style known as Isabelline. The mellow stone glows beautifully in the late afternoon sun, as the palace looks out, as it did in Diego's day, at ships arriving in the riverside port. These ships, including the cruise vessels that moor nearby, now dwarf the palace, but it must once have appeared much bigger to arriving sailors and traders.

Before moving to his palace, Diego had lived in the nearby **Casa del Cordón**, believed to have been built in 1500 and, as such, the oldest European two-storey building in the New World. The cord motif that gives the house its name is a reference to the influential Franciscan order of priests and can be seen in the sculpted image around the entrance. As well as serving as temporary accommodation for the governor, the building was home to an early court before the legal bureaucracy was transferred to Las Casas Reales.

City of firsts

As the first European city in the New World, Santo Domingo was inevitably the site of the first church, the first educational establishment and the first hospital in the Americas. The earliest church, properly speaking, was on the other side of the Ozama, and today a reconstructed single-nave chapel, the **Capilla del Rosario**, marks the spot of the original wooden church. Rebuilt in 1947, it is a small, plain church, overshadowed by the large multi-coloured grain silos nearby. Much more evocative of the heyday of Spanish

Casa del Cordón

colonial rule, however, are the many Catholic churches and institutions that decorate the narrow streets of the *zona colonial*. All of these religious buildings had the misfortune of being vandalised by the aggressively anti-Catholic Drake, although most have been restored over the centuries.

The Cathedral

Santo Domingo's cathedral, or to give it its full name the **Catedral Basílica Menor de Santa María**, dominates the *zona colonial*, its impressive stature testimony to the religious faith and ideology of the early colonists. According to some historians, Diego Colón personally laid the first foundation stone in 1514, although others believe that work began in 1521. In any event, the cathedral was completed in 1540 and inaugurated two years later, although a planned steeple never materialised due to shortage of funds. The cathedral reveals a curious mix of architectural styles, with classical arches and Gothic vaults competing with the ornate style known as the Plateresque, involving intricate allegorical sculptures and friezes. While the northern façade is massive and fortified, the western façade is an extravaganza of cherubs and mythical creatures along with frescoes of saints. Inside there are 14 separate side chapels, some commemorating early dignitaries such as Oviedo, Rodrigo de Bastidas and Bishop Alejandro Geraldini, an Italian-born cleric who had a hand in designing the cathedral.

Little of the original interior survived the attentions of Drake, who smashed much of the religious ornamentation while using the building as a headquarters and impromptu barracks. The English pirate even removed the stonework from around the bell tower, hence the exposed bricks. Yet successive waves of restoration work, most recently to coincide with the Columbus quincentenary, have succeeded in recreating the cathedral's colonial splendour. In one such period of restoration in 1877

◀ The restored façade

workmen reputedly found the remains of Christopher Columbus, and he was re-interred beneath the large and elaborate mausoleum behind the main altar before being removed to the Columbus Lighthouse in 1992. A chapel within the cathedral also commemorates Pope John Paul II's visit to the Dominican Republic in that year. The stained glass windows are mostly modern, by the Dominican Rincón Mora, but there are also several venerable treasures, not least the eighteenth-century mahogany altar and work by the Spanish artist Murillo. The main doors are original, made of mahogany, and are apparently locked at night with a 500-year-old key.

The southern door leads out of the cathedral and into the **Callejón de Curas** (Priests' Alley), leading to cloisters and the priests' living quarters. There was once a cemetery here, but that, like much else, was demolished by Drake. One of his cannonballs also killed Francisco Tostado, the poet and son of the writer of the same name, whose house, the **Casa Tostado**, stands a block away from the cathedral. Tostado senior was a contemporary of Oviedo, and his house dates from 1503; his unfortunate son is reputed to have written the first sonnet in the Americas. The house is remarkable for a double Gothic window – the only one in the Western hemisphere.

Religious buildings are thick on the ground in the *zona colonial*. One block further west, moving away from the river, is the impressively solid **Convento de los Dominicos**, a convent that was founded in 1510 and given university status in 1538 on the strength of its theology lectures. This promotion made it the first university in the Americas,

▲ Heraldic paving

although today's successor institution, the **Universidad Autónoma de Santo Domingo**, is some way away in the purpose-built Zona Universitaria campus. The Convento's Capilla del Rosario has a remarkably eclectic ceiling design, mixing a pagan zodiac wheel with classical gods and Christian saints in a bizarre synthesis of beliefs and periods.

Predictably, what is left of the first monastery in the Americas is also to be found in this area, a couple of blocks west of the Plaza España. The **Monasterio de San Francisco** was built in 1508, only to be levelled by Drake and then destroyed by two earthquakes in 1673 and 1751. After a series of restorations, the patched up building finally saw service as a lunatic asylum (there are brackets set into the walls for leg chains) and a laundry. Nowadays the ruins are used for cultural events, and the only recognisably monastic remains are the entrance with the Franciscan cord symbol above it and some atmospheric (and post-Drake) cloisters.

Nuns, too, had a claim to originality, as the **Iglesia Santa Clara** stands on the site of the hemisphere's first nunnery, not surprisingly demolished by the thoroughly anti-papist Drake. It was rebuilt with Spanish funding, and today a simple whitewashed Renaissance-style church, with a small school attached, marks the spot of the original institution.

San Nicolás de Bari Hospital

Churches often went hand in hand with charity in colonial Santo Domingo, and several remaining buildings recall how religious orders were obliged to take care of the sick and dying. The ruined **Hospital de San Nicolás de Bari** was constructed under the orders of Governor Ovando in 1503 as the first hospital in the Americas. Its patients were accommodated in wards adjacent to a central chapel, the whole building designed in the shape of a cross. It survived Drake's best efforts but finally became unsafe after a ferocious hurricane in 1911, and the city authorities decided to demolish most of the building to avoid masonry falling on unsuspecting passers-by. Nowadays the site presents an atmospheric and rather melancholic scene of Moorish arches and crumbling brick walls, enlivened by the presence of a huge colony of pigeons.

Other churches in the *zona colonial* also had a charitable and medical role. The Gothic **Iglesia de San Lázaro**, dating from 1650, was attached to a hospice for those suffering from leprosy, tuberculosis and other infectious diseases, while the **Iglesia de San Miguel** was supposed to offer care and solace to those afflicted by smallpox.

As well as charity, the Church was concerned with issues of defence, and several religious buildings have a strongly fortified look, not least the **Iglesia de Santa Bárbara**, on the northern wall of the colonial city. This ungainly building was inevitably damaged by Drake and then flattened by a hurricane before being rebuilt in the seventeenth century. A ruined fort is adjoined, and the church – dedicated to the patron saint of the military – seems sturdy enough to withstand another attack.

The *zona colonial* is, of course, a fortified community, a network of walls and forts running around its circumference. Gateways and towers show how the Spanish colonists attempted (and failed) to protect their settlement from attack from the river and sea, and many forts, mostly dating from the seventeenth century, have been restored and blend into the rest of the network of narrow streets, churches and single-storey colonial-era homes. The most interesting gateway is the **Puerta de la Misericordia** (Mercy Gate), to the west of the *zona colonial* and once the main entrance from that direction. First built in the 1540s, this stout structure apparently sheltered citizens from falling masonry during a particularly destructive earthquake in 1842. It was also here that the nationalists of La Trinitaria began their uprising against the Haitian occupiers two years later.

▲ The Mercy Gate

81

Puerta del Conde

Shopping streets

The **Puerta del Conde**, a seventeenth-century stone and brick construction dedicated to Count Bracamonte, who beat off another British invasion attempt in 1655, marks the western entrance into the colonial city. It stands by **Parque Independencia**, a peaceful open space amidst the hubbub of the traffic-dominated meeting of several large streets. Here, the **Altar de la Patria** contains the remains of independence heroes, Duarte, Sánchez and Mella in a solemn mausoleum, and the park itself is remembered as the patriotic site where the Dominican flag was first raised in 1844.

From this park to the Parque Colón, the heart of the *zona colonial*, a straight pedestrian-only street, the **Calle El Conde**, cuts through the old town on its way down to the river. This broad commercial thoroughfare is always busy, lined by shops selling clothes, shoes and music and filled with vendors and hustlers of every type. Avoid the dishonest money-changers but enjoy the sheer buzz of Santo Domingo's everyday urban life. Most of the buildings are of recent construction, and El Conde is more North American than Spanish in appearance, but it is worth walking its length to view crowds of smartly dressed locals on a permanent shopping spree. At the other end, the quiet charm of the tree-filled **Parque Colón**, bordered on one side by the cathedral and surrounded by ornate public buildings, is a welcome contrast. Here stands a statue of Christopher Columbus, the explorer theatrically pointing to some unspecified land with a half naked Taino maiden at his feet.

If El Conde is busy, then the **Avenida Mella**, the long artery that runs down from the main bridge over the Ozama to join the Parque Independencia, is simply frantic. A concrete jungle of gaudy hoardings, hooting traffic and human congestion makes this popular shopping street something of a challenge, but there are bargains in clothes, cameras and liquor to be had in the huge array of emporia. Some shops, known as *botánicas*, specialise in religious icons and voodoo artefacts, mixing plaster cast saints with exotic potions and spells. In the heart of the shopping mayhem lies the **Mercado Modelo**, a covered bazaar of traders offering ornaments and items of every possible description. This seething marketplace and the run-down streets around is the centre of Santo Domingo's Haitian community, transient and fixed, and their presence is reflected in the colourful Haitian paintings and African-influenced carvings on sale.

Suburban charm

Only a few blocks away from the frenzy of Avenida Mella, heading westwards along Avenida Bolívar, is the quiet residential district of **Gazcue**. This is the first and the oldest of the various middle-class suburbs that spread out from the colonial centre in the nineteenth and twentieth centuries. Gazcue, with its wide tree-lined streets and verdant gardens, was especially popular in the 1930s and 1940s during the heyday of the Trujillo dictatorship, and many of the comfortable homes belonged to supporters of the regime. Nowadays, there are small hotels, restaurants and art galleries dotted among the leafy streets. It was here that Trujillo decided to locate his pink neoclassical **Palacio Nacional** or presidential palace, complete with dome and portico. The building can be visited, even though it is still often used by the president.

Statue in Gazcue

Presidential Palace

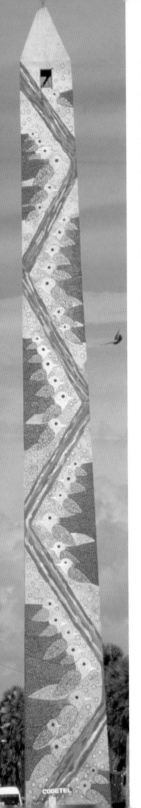

Further along the crowded **Avenida Bolívar** lies another presidential monument, this time constructed under the aegis of Joaquín Balaguer during the economic boom of the 1970s. The modern **Plaza de la Cultura** is an impressive complex of theatre, art museum, history and ethnology museums and library, housed in functional, if not, beautiful, concrete blocks (the attractive marble theatre is the exception and has a sumptuous interior). The **Museo de Arte Moderno** contains a permanent exhibition of modern Dominican art, ranging from pastoral oil paintings to challenging avant-garde works. Jaime Colson and José Vela Zanetti, the two modern artists most associated with the Dominican Republic, are well represented. Nearby, the **Museo del Hombre Dominicano** (Museum of Dominican Man) has a fascinating display of Taino objects and also explains a good deal about African influences in Dominican rural life and religion. The **Museo de Historia y Geografia** is perhaps rather less interesting, especially in its propagandising approach to Haiti and its nineteenth-century occupation, but there are extraordinary insights to be gleaned into the character of Trujillo, including his makeup set, used to disguise his own allegedly Haitian complexion.

West of the Plaza de la Cultura the city spreads out in a North American-style pattern of shopping malls, intersecting highways and office complexes. Skyscrapers, once rare, are becoming slightly more common, especially around the big commercial centres, but there are still many green spaces and quiet residential areas. These affluent districts stand in stark contrast to the squalid shanty towns to be found on the edge of the city and on the banks of the Ozama.

The Malecón

Santo Domingo is a city girdled by water, both river and sea, and the long **Avenida George Washington**, invariably known as the *Malecón*, is its waterside boulevard. Many of the capital's plushest hotels line this road, looking out to sea, while there are also a

◀ Obelisk on the *Malecón*

great many bars and restaurants. The **Ciudad Nueva** district, adjacent to the *zona colonial*, is the most atmospheric part of the seaside city, with rather run-down nineteenth-century architecture and little plazas where locals sit and chat in the evening. On the water's edge stands the gigantic statue of Antón de Montesinos, the turbulent priest who condemned the genocide of the Tainos. Donated by the Mexican government, it dwarfs the nearby houses. As the road winds around the coast, there are many shaded places to sit, outdoor bars, and rocky outcrops where hopeful fishermen try their luck.

In its two-mile trajectory, the *Malecón* has other monumental landmarks. Two obelisks were erected by Trujillo in honour of himself, although one has been painted to commemorate the Mirabal sisters who were among his victims. It was along this coastal road, incidentally, that Trujillo met his end in an ambush of his car. Nowadays, the *Malecón* is more associated with music than murder, for it is here that the annual merengue festival takes place each summer, turning the road into what the *Guinness Book of Records* has termed 'the planet's largest disco'.

▼ The Columbus Lighthouse

Across the Ozama

Most of Santo Domingo's sights and attractions are to be found on the west side of the river, but recent developments have given interest to the eastern side. The most controversial of these was the construction of the vast – and to many rather ugly – **Faro a Colón** (Columbus Lighthouse), whose grey silhouette is easily visible from far away. Built to mark the 1992 anniversary, the lighthouse inspired intense opposition because of its reputed $150-million cost and because a crowded shanty town was bulldozed to make way for it. Even the powerful beam of light it projects into the night sky was criticised in a city where electric light was – and still is – an unreliable luxury for the poor.

85

The marble-clad concrete structure, in the shape of a recumbent cross, was designed in the 1920s by a British architecture student for an international competition, but the plans were not put into action until the late 1980s. In the centre is Columbus' mausoleum, a baroque construction permanently guarded by a Dominican sailor, and there is also a chapel and various rooms for exhibitions. The building is surrounded by a manicured park, clearly a far cry from the busy community that existed here before. While the entire venture has been criticised as an inappropriate use of funds in a poor country, there is no doubt that the sight of the projected light playing on night-time clouds is an impressive spectacle. Many Dominicans, however, view the lighthouse with suspicion, as tainted by the curse of Columbus.

Elsewhere on the east bank, the government is planning to develop the area known as **Sans Souci** with a marina, cruise ship terminal and even a convention centre. The area is also due to feature in the 2004 Pan American Games, to be held in Santo Domingo. This riverside district borders the **Parque Mirador del Este**, in which the Columbus Lighthouse is situated. At the eastern end of the park is a complex of four (despite the name) water-filled caves known as **Los Tres Ojos**. Believed to have been public baths in Taino times, the freshwater sinkholes, one of which is particularly sulphurous, are reached by a staircase carved into the limestone. From here it is a short taxi ride to the National Aquarium, with its underwater walkway and appealing orphaned manatee.

Los Tres Ojos

❻ Mountains and rivers
The Cibao and Cordillera Central

After the frantic urban pace of Santo Domingo, an exploration of the Dominican Republic's mountainous interior provides a welcome contrast. Far from the sweltering atmosphere of the south coast, the chain of hills and mountains that makes up the spine of the country offers cool temperatures by day and even frost at night. The **Cordillera Central** mountain range is an area of outstanding natural beauty, with impressive peaks and densely forested hillsides cut by lush valleys and fast flowing rivers. To the east and watered by rivers that descend from the mountains is the **Cibao**, the most fertile part of the country and traditionally its agricultural heartland. Here are the most prosperous farming communities in the Dominican Republic and its second city, **Santiago de Los Caballeros**.

North of Santo Domingo

Leaving behind the sprawling northern industrial suburbs of Santo Domingo, the country's main highway, the Autopista Duarte, winds its way through flat countryside before the first mountains of the Cordillera Central begin to appear to the west. The road is invariably busy, with an eclectic mix of modern vehicles, carts and animals, while much commercial activity takes place on the roadside. The first major town is **Bonao**, a bleak and uninviting mining community that depends for its livelihood on the nearby Canadian-owned Falconbridge nickel mine, noticeable from a distance by its large chimneys. Bonao has little to offer the visitor apart from an art centre, founded by the Bonao-born painter, Cándido Bido, whose colourful scenes of rural life are on view here as well as in chic galleries in Santo Domingo.

▼ La Vega

The next sizeable conurbation is **La Vega**, another industrial town of some 200 000 people but with more to recommend it than Bonao. There are some pretty early twentieth-century buildings among the modern concrete streets, but the most conspicuous structure is the 1992 cathedral, a strange castle-like building that looks like something from a film set. Remembered as the birthplace of the veteran politician Juan Bosch, La Vega is also famous for its annual carnival celebrations, involving music and costumed devils.

▼ Carnival mask

La Vega's real significance, however, is historical, for the original settlement (known now as La Vega Vieja), a little to the north of the modern town, was founded by Christopher Columbus in 1494 as a base for mining what he thought were the vast gold deposits in the surrounding valley. This early settlement became an important town, with a cathedral and its own bishop, but was flattened by an earthquake in 1562. Little remains of this colonial outpost apart from the walls of a fortress and some foundations. The nearby **Santo Cerro** (Holy Hill) also owes its reputation to Columbus, for it is claimed that when, in 1495, the Spanish were involved in a battle against insurgent Tainos, a miracle occurred. As the Tainos attempted for some reason to burn a large wooden cross that Columbus had personally erected on the hillside, it refused to catch fire. The Virgin Mary is then said to have appeared sitting on the cross, terrifying the Tainos and giving courage to the beleaguered Spanish. The site of this event now attracts crowds of pilgrims each year on 24 September to a nineteenth-century church on the hilltop, from where there are vast and spectacular views over the fertile Vega Real valley.

Santo Cerro

The Dominican Alps

A left turn shortly after leaving La Vega northwards on the Autopista takes the traveller up a windy road through thick pine forests to the town of **Jarabacoa**. This is a popular spot with the wealthier inhabitants of Santo Domingo, some of whom escape to second homes in the cool mountain air. The town itself is pleasant but unexceptional, with modern buildings outnumbering older houses. The appeal lies more in the surrounding countryside,

▲ Jarabacoa landscape

dubbed the Dominican Alps on account of fresh air, pine forests and mountain views. The climate allows for a wide range of agriculture, and the region around Jarabacoa is famous for growing strawberries, coffee and ornamental flowers for export. Nowadays, tourism is a big part of Jarabacoa's economic well-being, and small hotels, ranches and camping accommodation are dotted around the town and the surrounding region.

The main attractions in the vicinity are the rivers and waterfalls, particularly the **Río Yaque del Norte**, the country's longest river, and **El Salto de Jimenoa**, a 37-metre (120-foot) waterfall that cascades into a rocky pool below. You can swim in the pool, and access to the falls is via a wobbly suspension bridge that hangs over the spray below. Several other falls are accessible, but only by long walks or four-wheel drive vehicles. One of them, further down the Jimenoa River on the road to Constanza, is a torrent of water dropping over 60 metres (200 feet) down a sheer rock face onto huge boulders. So dramatic is the setting that it was reputedly used in the filming of *Jurassic Park*.

Jarabacoa is also one of the starting points for climbing the 3000-metre (9850 feet) **Pico Duarte**, with expeditions beginning at the village of **La Ciénaga**, some 20 kilometres (12 miles) west of the town. The two adjacent national parks, **Amando Bermúdez** and **José del Carmen Ramírez**, are close by, allowing walkers and wildlife enthusiasts access to some spectacular and unspoilt woodland (permits must always be obtained for entrance into the parks).

Higher still than Jarabacoa is the mountain town of **Constanza**, sitting in a lush crater-shaped valley at 1200 metres (3940 feet) above sea level. The road between the two is almost impassable, so it is better to approach Constanza from the turning after Bonao.

Like Jarabacoa, the scenery around is more impressive than the town itself, a nondescript grid of modern streets. Beyond the town, however, the views are stunning, encompassing rich green vistas of meadows, pine forests and the surrounding rim of mountains. Farming is the main commercial activity, with non-tropical crops such as strawberries and garlic grown for the domestic and export markets. The area's farming potential was recognised in the 1950s by Trujillo, who invited hundreds of Japanese immigrants to settle in special agricultural colonies. Nowadays, there are still Japanese-descended farmers in the area, but the run-down camp outside town, called Colonia Japonesa, is now home to impoverished seasonal farm workers from Haiti.

▼ Constanza Valley

Constanza's main natural attraction, about 10 kilometres (6 miles) south of the Colonia, is the **Agua Blanca** waterfall, 150 metres (492 feet) of cascading water that ends up in a large pool surrounded by rocky cliffs. The scenery around is a strange mix of vertiginous mountain slopes, cultivated terraces and farm buildings clinging on to steep hillsides. From here it is possible – in theory – to drive southwards through the Valle Nuevo National Park to San José de Ocoa. In practice, recent hurricane damage has made the already treacherous road through the remote mountain terrain impassable.

Farming land

On the other side of the Autopista Duarte lies the flat and fertile Cibao Valley, the place where Columbus dreamed of locating unheard-of supplies of gold. If the region disappointed the Spanish gold-hunters, it has nevertheless produced much prosperity since in the shape of rice, coffee, tobacco and cacao. This is the heartland of Dominican agriculture, the richest rural area, and the source of wealth for the traditional upper classes of Santiago. Large estates dominate here, and there are extensive paddy fields devoted to rice. Apart from Santiago, three towns dominate the Cibao, each acting as a centre for trading and

shopping for the farming communities. **San Francisco de Macorís** was famous in the nineteenth century as a tobacco town, but more recently has become associated with chocolate production, its **Mercado Modelo** acting as a vast depot for local cacao farmers. Rumour has it that much of the high-priced modern development on the outskirts is due to another profitable product – cocaine – but few questions are asked. A new and spacious baseball ground is testimony to the money that comes from San Franciscans overseas, some of whom are popularly reputed to be involved in drug smuggling.

▼ Agriculture in the Cibao Valley

West of San Francisco de Macorís lies the smaller town of **Salcedo**, known for its annual handicraft fair in the summer. The town is also famous as the birthplace of the Mirabal sisters, four young women from a prosperous family who were courageous opponents of the Trujillo dictatorship. Three of them were murdered on the orders of Trujillo in 1960, and they have subsequently become powerful symbols of political martyrdom and women's rights, celebrated not only on the obelisk on Santo Domingo's *Malecón* but in Julia Alvarez's acclaimed novel, *In the Time of the Butterflies* (1994). A small museum east of the town centre is located in the family home and contains memorabilia.

Turning westwards towards Santiago, the town of **Moca** lies amidst some of the country's best farming land. It is also remembered in Dominican history as the place where one of the country's most enduring dictators, Ulises Heureaux, was assassinated in 1899. The ordinary town centre is overshadowed by the large **Iglesia Corazón de Jesús** (Heart of Jesus Church), with elaborate stained glass windows and a tall clock tower that can be climbed.

Santiago

With a population of over 700 000, **Santiago** is a metropolis by Dominican standards, a commercial centre and important focus for the surrounding agricultural economy. Linked to the capital by the Autopista Duarte, it also has good connections to the north coast port of Puerto Plata. Many Santiago people view Santo Domingo with distaste, as a parasitic place of civil servants and bureaucrats, believing, with some justification, that the real money in the country is made in the old-fashioned rum and cigar industries. Many politicians and presidents have hailed from Santiago, and there is undisguised rivalry between this dynamic city and the larger capital. Santiago prides itself, for instance, on its merengue, especially the local *perico ripao* style, and there is healthy competition between baseball teams.

Santiago certainly has fewer architectural and historic treasures than Santo Domingo. Founded in 1495 by 30 Spanish notables (the *caballeros* of its full title), it started, like La Vega, as a centre for supervising forced gold mining in the Cibao Valley. This original settlement was flattened by an earthquake in 1562, and a new town was relocated on the eastern side of the Río Yaque del Norte. More disasters in the form of further earthquakes, pirate raids and fires blighted the city throughout the eighteenth and nineteenth centuries, and in 1805 the invading Haitians killed

▶ Santiago's landmark monument

most of the inhabitants. As a result, there is little of any great age to be found in the present-day city, its most interesting buildings dating from the nineteenth century. This was the period of Santiago's prosperity, as traders from Germany and the US bought the high-quality tobacco grown in the nearby hills. This boom is reflected in civic buildings such as the **Centro de Recreo**, an exclusive 1890s social club for the city's rum oligarchs complete with ornate ballroom and Moorish-inspired exterior, and the neoclassical cathedral, featuring modern stained glass windows, a mahogany altar and the tomb of the assassinated dictator Heureaux. Both these buildings border the central and shaded **Parque Duarte**.

Another dictator left his mark on the city in the shape of the huge **Monumento a los Héroes de la Restauración**. This 70-metre (230 feet) pillar standing on a white marble temple-like base is topped by a statue of Victory and was originally commissioned by Trujillo to commemorate his own achievements. Upon his death it was rededicated to those who had died in the struggle to wrest independence from Spain in 1863. Trujillo's intention, it was said, was to impose on Santiago a landmark – and by implication a reminder of his power – that could be seen from all parts of the city. In this he undoubtedly succeeded. It is possible to climb to a viewing position at the top of the tower, from where the city,

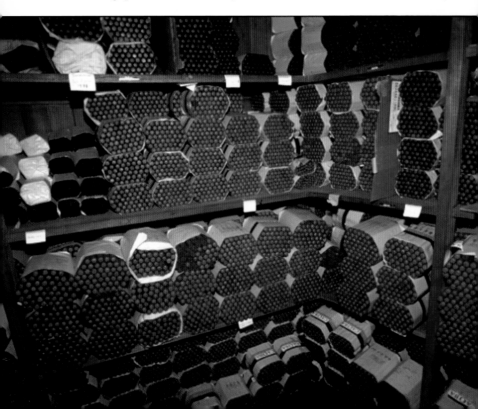

mountains and plain spread out beneath one's feet. At weekends the open space around the monument is popular with locals, especially younger people, and open-air bars and merengue music help create a noisy party atmosphere. This is where Santiago's celebrated carnival celebrations culminate on 27 February. Just behind the tower is the imposing marble **Gran Teatro del Cibao**, built by Trujillo's one-time confidant Joaquín Balaguer in the 1980s.

Santiago's vibrant commercial role is clearly visible in the central shopping street, the **Calle del Sol**, a slightly less frantic version of Santo Domingo's Avenida Mella. Here, too, advertising hoardings, music and crowds can create a formidable assault on the nerves of the inexperienced shopper. The two essentials (for smokers and drinkers) to be bought in Santiago are cigars and rum, both locally produced by centuries-old techniques. The **Tabacos Don Esteban cigar factory** is open to visitors on the road out of town towards Santo Domingo. Demonstrations of cigar rolling are on offer as well as quality cigars. The **Bermúdez rum factory** can also be visited; this is to be found in the northwestern Pueblo Nuevo suburb. Staff will be pleased to show off the distilling and bottling process and to offer some samples of the venerable aged rum.

◀ Cigars for sale

❼ The tourist trail
The north coast

The north coast was where the Dominican Republic's tourism boom really began. From the 1960s, travellers began to discover the long sandy beaches and small towns that make up this area, thus putting into motion a process of development that has transformed the so-called **Amber Coast** around Puerto Plata out of recognition. Nowadays, large tourist complexes vie with low-budget apartments, top-class windsurfers arrive on the same flight as family holiday-makers, and the old industries of sugarcane and fishing give way to the onward march of tourism.

Not that all of the north coast is dominated by tourism. There are still sleepy towns like Monte Cristi, where visitors are few and far between, and large parts of the Samaná Peninsula are yet to be developed. But around Puerto Plata in particular, the mark of mass tourism has been unmistakable. This has brought prosperity to some communities that had previously had few economic opportunities, but it has also had its downside in the shape of unregulated development and sudden social change.

Puerto Plata

Puerto Plata, the 'silver port', was so named by Christopher Columbus in 1493 on account of the glittering water he saw in the bay. The forest-clad mountain that stood guard over the bay he named Mount Isabel de Torres in a sensible gesture of deference to the Spanish queen who had bankrolled his expedition. It became an important early colonial settlement, founded in 1502 by Governor Nicolás de Ovando, and at first earned its living by offering protection and supplies to Spanish ships returning with their loads of silver from Mexico to Spain. The steady flow of treasure galleons attracted the attention of pirates, who dreamed of capturing a silver-filled vessel, and the colonial authorities were obliged to build the sturdy Fortaleza de San Felipe in 1540 as a deterrent to pirate raids.

Gradually, however, Puerto Plata's fortunes faded as Havana seemed to provide a safer haven, and the town fell into decline, trading with the dubious merchants and privateers who frequented the wild north coast. Eventually, the Spanish grew tired of foreign encroachments into their coastal territory and in 1605 effectively shut Puerto Plata and other settlements down, forcing the inhabitants to move to Santo Domingo. For a century and a half the area around Puerto Plata was a lawless, largely uninhabited wilderness, home to buccaneers and other undesirables.

The city of Puerto Plata was rebuilt and resettled in the mid-eighteenth century when the Spanish, threatened by the growth of the French colony of Saint Domingue, decided to reassert their presence on the north coast. The port was renovated and new immigrants, mostly from the Canary Islands, were encouraged to settle. In its new guise, Puerto Plata became the export centre for the commodities – timber, sugar and later tobacco – originating from the Cibao Valley and Santiago. Its heyday came in the latter

▼ Gingerbread style

▲ Former glories

part of the nineteenth century, when German tobacco merchants and their local partners invested heavily in warehouses, offices and prosperous-looking homes. But this boom was short-lived, as the US occupation drove the Germans away.

The long Trujillo dictatorship made things worse, as Trujillo distrusted Puerto Plata's vocal opposition groups and punished the city by locking up its most prominent citizens and starving it of investment. The completion of the Autopista Duarte between Santiago and Santo Domingo in 1922 had been another blow, as the port was no longer the only export conduit for Cibao goods.

For most of the twentieth century Puerto Plata gently stagnated. It was only with a brief sugar boom in the 1960s and the beginnings of tourism at the same time that its fortunes began to revive. Even today, though, there is a rather run-down and melancholic feel about the old town, with its often decrepit Victorian mansions and

▶ Puerto Plata shops

▲ Playa Dorada

rotting warehouses. While it is the biggest urban centre on the north coast, with more than 200 000 inhabitants, and has an international airport and cruise ship dock, it is not in itself a tourist magnet, as most visitors tend to congregate in the nearby purpose-built complex of Playa Dorada. Even so, this historically interesting city is worth a visit.

The limestone **Fortaleza de San Felipe**, overlooking the bay from a promontory, is the only structure to have survived the evacuation of 1605, although it has been much renovated over the last century. The cannons, thick walls, turrets and moat are all evidence of its strategic importance, but more sinister are the cramped rooms that served as prison cells for most of the fort's history. Pablo Duarte, the father of Dominican independence, was held here in 1844, while Trujillo's secret police kept political opponents in the underground cells in the 1950s and 1960s. Among them were the husbands of the Mirabal sisters, and it was after visiting their menfolk in the fortress that the three sisters were murdered on Trujillo's orders in 1960. The cells are open to the public, and a small museum tells the story of Puerto Plata's turbulent past.

The promontory has been cleaned up because of the nearby cruise ship terminal, and there are good views over the bay and the Atlantic. A large equestrian statue of General Gregorio Luperón, a Puerto Plata-born hero in the struggle against the Spanish colonial regime in the 1860s and then a president, rears

◀ Fortaleza de San Felipe, Puerto Plata

up with its back to the sea. Less well preserved is a rusting metal lighthouse, built in 1879 and a protected monument, but slowly falling apart due to neglect and salty sea breezes.

▲ Glorieta, Puerto Plata

The heart of the old town is the **Parque Independencia** (known locally as the *Parque Central*), a tree-lined open space decorated by a restored green-and-white Victorian gazebo or *glorieta*. Around the square are the best and most sensitively renovated examples of Victorian architecture, pastel-coloured wooden structures of shaded arcades and balconies embellished with the fancy fretwork known as gingerbread style. The imposing two-towered **Catedral San Felipe** is a renovated mix of Art Deco and traditional colonial styles but is rather uninteresting inside. The main attraction in the centre of town is rather the **Museo del Ambar** (Amber Museum), housed on Avenida Duarte in the beautiful former residence of a wealthy German tobacco merchant. Here is an exhibition of the valuable solidified resin mined in the mountains of the Cordillera Septentrional, the range that separates Puerto Plata from Santiago. Many of the exhibits, which range from golden and red to green and blue, contain fossilised insects, leaves and flowers. Visitors can inspect raw amber as well as examples of the jewellery that has become a speciality of the Dominican Republic.

▶ Amber

▲ Catedral San Felipe

▲ Puerto Plata cable car

Outside the small grid system of the old town the newer *barrios* spread eastwards in a mix of industrial complexes and poor residential neighbourhoods. The seafront *Malecón* runs for a mile or so, but the beach is dirty and there is little to attract the visitor except in October when this boulevard hosts the annual Merengue Festival. To the east of the town, near the baseball stadium, is the **Brugal rum factory**, where rum is bottled rather than actually produced. This installation welcomes visitors and offers samples of various rum cocktails.

To the west is the cable car that carries passengers on a vertiginous 25-minute ride to the top of the 800-metre (2627 feet) **Isabel de Torres** mountain. The cable car has suffered from

▲ Christ statue, Pico Isabel de Torres

mechanical problems in recent years and service is not always reliable, but if running, it allows visitors an extraordinary view of the city, coastline and sea from a pretty mountaintop site. A statue of Christ, similar to but smaller than the effigy in Rio de Janeiro, looks down on the expanse of north coast scenery, and there are cafés and souvenir shops.

Beach resorts

The rather faded charms of Puerto Plata stand in contrast to the luxurious facilities on show at the beach resorts on either side of the city. To the west lie the beaches of **Costambar** and **Cofresí**, each with a choice of hotels and apartments together with shopping malls and water sport centres. Only a couple of miles east of Puerto Plata's suburbs, meanwhile, is the resort of **Playa Dorada**, a large self-contained holiday complex containing almost 5000 hotel rooms. This modern development encompasses a golf course as well as discos, casinos and a large range of restaurants and bars. Indeed, so extensive are the attractions that many tourists are happy to remain within the confines of the complex rather than venture out to Puerto Plata or beyond.

If so, they miss the spectacular scenery that extends eastwards down the Amber Coast as it follows bays, headlands and beaches to meet the protruding peninsula of Samaná. Some of this coastline is now developed, villas and condominiums sitting in suburban gardens, but much remains empty and sometimes wild. Its backdrop is one of mountains, tumbling down to the coastal plain, and its beaches are as often as not lined by palm trees.

The coast is dotted by small towns, some of which have learnt to live with tourism and share in a new-found prosperity. The town of **Sosúa**, for instance, was an obscure fishing village until the 1980s, when it was rapidly transformed into a tourist centre of

Sosúa

hotels, restaurants and discos. It remains a lively place, buzzing with nightlife, and boasts a pretty kilometre-long beach on a horseshoe bay.

▲ Sosúa's popular beach

▼ Sosúa synagogue

Its historic claim to fame predates the tourist boom, however, and goes back to the 1940s when Trujillo, eager to attract European immigrants to the Dominican Republic, offered asylum to Jewish victims of Nazi persecution, funded by US sympathisers. Sosúa, which had previously been a trans-shipment point for the US United Fruit Company's banana plantations but abandoned since 1916, seemed an obvious place for a new Jewish colony. Several hundred European migrants duly arrived and founded a *barrio*, El Batey, to the east of the bay. After unsuccessful attempts to compete with local peasants in vegetable production, the colonists set up a cooperative dairy, producing milk, cheese and meat products. The venture was a success and Sosúa's Jews established a wooden synagogue, which is still in operation in the El Batey district. Next door is a museum that tells the story of the Jewish cooperative. Although there are still descendants of the original settlers in Sosúa, the community has largely disappeared through migration and intermarriage. The dairy is still a going concern, however, and the one-room synagogue continues to attract a small number of faithful.

Around the headland of Cabo Macorís, the windsurfing paradise of **Cabarete** is a different world from the crowded sands of Sosúa. Trade winds produce the monster waves that sweep towards the beach in the afternoons, attracting windsurfers from around the world to take part in international competitions. For those unwilling to participate in Cabarete's *macho* surfing culture, it

▲ Cabarete

is reassuring to know that an international sandcastle building contest takes place here every February. The town itself is a strip of recent developments, backing on to a large lagoon with extensive wild bird life. There was no tourism here until the 1980s, but now the rows of condominiums, restaurants and water sport shops testify to the astronomical growth in foreign visitors.

The same future probably awaits the attractive small town of **Río San Juan**, some 80 kilometres (50 miles) east of Puerto Plata. Still a quiet community of fishermen and boat builders, this *pueblo* is beginning to attract tourists, especially along the idyllic **Playa Grande**. Its main attraction is a lagoon, the **Laguna Gri-Gri,** which is almost within the town itself and which can be visited by boat for views of thick mangrove and a cave inhabited by a flock of swallows.

▼ Playa Grande

⚠ Ramshackle building on the Samaná Peninsula

The Samaná Peninsula

The Samaná Peninsula, jutting out into the Atlantic Ocean, may seem a quiet and remote backwater, but it was once the subject of intense superpower rivalry over its strategic importance. The real target for the US and Germany in particular was the bay that lies to the south of the peninsula, for this stretch of water, protected on three sides, is one of the finest natural harbours in the Caribbean. Early Dominican presidents were aware of its appeal to nations with navies that needed shelter during the hurricane season, and several attempts were made by unscrupulous *caudillos* to sell or lease Samaná Bay as a naval base or coaling station to the US. When Germany showed an interest in setting up a military base there, it precipitated the US occupation of 1916, as the Americans were not prepared to let their European rivals establish a foothold in the region. Even before then, Columbus had had a violent encounter with some local indigenous warriors in 1493, while Napoleon Bonaparte reportedly considered setting up a vast French military complex around the bay.

Nowadays the placid port of **Samaná**, overlooking the bay and a couple of small islands, seems far removed from such excitement. Little happens in this small town, which was founded in the 1750s and settled by immigrants imported from the Canary Islands. A fire in 1946 damaged many of the original buildings, and worse was to happen when President Joaquín Balaguer, himself a native of the region, decided to turn the town into a tourist centre. With foreign aid, he removed the surviving older buildings and replaced them with modern, concrete architecture, wide roads and a couple of resorts. The causeway to the islands in the bay dates from this ill-advised piece of tourist development. But the tourists never came, and Samaná has remained quiet (apart from the incessant buzz of *motoconcho* taxis). The main attraction is the **Cayo**

Levantado, an islet of white sand and majestic palms reached by a regular ferry service from Samaná's waterfront.

One building in town is of some historic interest; the white, tin-roofed church in the centre of town is known as **La Churcha**, its English-sounding name a reminder that it was set up by Methodists for use by African-American settlers who arrived in the Samaná district in the 1820s. They had been invited by the Haitian authorities during Haiti's occupation of the eastern part of Hispaniola, and received the support of groups in the US who wanted to help blacks escape from the racism of the southern states. Many ended up in and around Samaná, and there is still evidence of their presence in family names, customs and a local English dialect.

Despite Balaguer's ambitions for the town of Samaná, the tourists who come to the peninsula are more likely to head for the idyllic north coast resorts of **Las Galeras** and **Las Terrenas**. Beaches like **Playa Rincón**, close to Las Galeras and nestling in a horseshoe cove, are among the best in the country and yet are, as yet, uncrowded. Until relatively recently, these villages, surrounded by long sandy beaches and coconut groves, were virtually unknown to the wider world. Today, however, an influx of expatriates from North America and Europe has created several communities of tourism-oriented growth, with guesthouses, restaurants and bars lining the once-deserted beaches.

Much of this development is small-scale, but bigger hotels have also arrived in Las Galeras and Las Terrenas, encouraged by the airport at El Portillo, which welcomes charter flights as well as private planes. Those who do not arrive in such style normally come by road via the formerly busy port of **Sánchez**, now a rather run-down town whose only reminders of its heyday in the early twentieth century are some ornate Victorian gingerbread residences.

▼ Empty beach near Samaná

West of Puerto Plata

The coastline stretching westwards towards the Haitian border is less developed than the eastern side, but contains some sites of considerable historical interest. Passing through the small resorts of Costambar and Cofresí, the traveller is faced with a choice of poor roads, perhaps the better option being to turn southwards to the small town of Imbert and from there to drive inland towards Monte Cristi. Small roads run along the coast, passing through tiny seaside villages, although many

 La Isabela's cemetery

of these are extremely rudimentary. The only town of any size between Puerto Plata and Monte Cristi is **Luperón**, a remote outpost that has a single large hotel outside town and little else. The beaches around are mostly empty.

▼ Luperón

From Luperón a good road runs west to the remains of Columbus' first settlement, La Isabela, the ill-fated camp that was evacuated in 1496. Now the centrepiece of a historic national park, the site contains the stone foundations of several buildings and a cemetery looking out to sea. Legend has it that when the dictator Trujillo ordered that the place be tidied up for the visit of some dignitaries, the workmen misunderstood and simply bulldozed the uncovered remnants into the sea. A small museum has artefacts of Taino and early colonial life, while the nearby **Templo de las Américas** is a modern church, built in 1992 for the Pope's visit to the place where the first Mass in the Americas was celebrated.

Wild and undeveloped beaches are plentiful in the northwest corner of the Republic, but many are hard to reach without a four-wheel drive vehicle. The landscape changes west of La Isabela, as fertile farmland and forest gives way to an arid semi-desert of cactus and thorns. Temperatures here are very high and rainfall scarce,

▲ La Isabela's museum

producing a dry and inhospitable countryside with only occasional small *pueblos*.

At the end of the road is the dusty town of **Monte Cristi**, a place with the atmosphere of a spaghetti western film set. Set in the flat hot delta of the Río Yaque del Norte with only the flat-topped El Morro mountain to break the monotony, the town lives in a time

▼ Monte Cristi

warp, its well-preserved Victorian architecture reflecting its golden age as an export conduit for timber, salt and rice. The first settlement here was founded in 1533, but it was abandoned in 1606 and then refounded by Canary Island immigrants in the mid-eighteenth century. Situated at the mouth of the river, it was a good place for exporting goods from Santiago that were ferried downstream, and the town flourished until it was all but destroyed in the 1860s Restoration War against the Spanish. The gingerbread mansions around the main square date from its rebuilding and another brief boom when a railway line linked it to the Cibao Valley.

No boom seems imminent these days, as local people make a modest living from goat farming and salt production. What tourism there is revolves around the nearby national park, situated in the delta and home to extensive mangroves and wetlands. From Monte Cristi it is also easy to reach the border town of **Dajabón**, one of several bustling markets where Dominicans and Haitians trade together. Each Monday and Friday this frontier town comes alive as Haitian traders sell everything from plastic utensils to counterfeit jeans in a hot and noisy open-air bazaar.

⑧ Sugar and sand
The east

In contrast to the mountainous north and the inhospitable west, the east of the Dominican Republic is made up of rolling plains and prime ranching land. This is the area where the first big estates were carved out by the Spanish colonists and where cattle first roamed the open spaces of the new colony. It is also the part of the Dominican Republic that has been most intensively farmed for sugarcane, the centre of an industry that has brought both riches and poverty to the country. Even today, sugar dominates the region's main towns – La Romana and San Pedro de Macorís – where the tall chimneys of sugar mills and the squalid encampments of Haitian cane-cutters are a reminder of the crop's historic grip on the Dominican people.

Yet just as sugar determined the country's fate in the nineteenth century, so tourism, the modern-day economic lifeblood, is much in evidence. The beaches that stretch from Santo Domingo eastwards along the Caribbean Sea (the Costa del Caribe) began to attract an international clientele from the 1980s onwards but before then were popular with the people of Santo Domingo, who have no decent sand of their own. Now, the coastline that runs up the eastern tip of the country (the Costa del Coco) is vying for economic supremacy as huge new developments at Punta Cana and Bávaro mark the latest phase in Dominican tourism.

The gulf between the coastal resorts and the sleepy farming towns of the interior is enormous, reflecting the different worlds that exist in today's Dominican Republic. It also helps to explain the appeal of this region, in which the traditional and the modern successfully co-exist.

The Caribbean coast

East of Santo Domingo the modern highway soon clears the suburban sprawl to bypass the airport and head out towards the seaside resorts which have traditionally served the capital's population on weekends and holidays. The first is **Boca Chica**, 30 kilometres

▶ Costa del Caribe

(19 miles) from Santo Domingo, more a concentration of tourist facilities than a community as such, although three decades ago this was a small fishing village popular with wealthier Dominicans who could afford a weekend retreat. Its proximity to the city has enhanced its popularity among all classes of Dominicans these days, and on weekends the town is invaded by holiday-makers and all those who aim to make money from them. Congested and noisy, Boca Chica may appeal to those who like crowds, but the level of hustling and *motoconcho* noise is too high for most tastes. The reason people come is the beach, a gently sloping stretch of sand leading to placid waters. Some of it is fenced off by hotels, the rest occupied by a mix of locals, foreigners and touts.

Further along the coast, the similarly tourism-oriented resort of **Juan Dolio** comprises a strip of hotels and other facilities along the beach. Dating from the 1980s, Juan Dolio was one of the first Dominican experiments in all-inclusive hotels and, as such, is not a true community but rather an enclave for foreigners. The beach has been criticised as unsafe and uncomfortable due to broken coral, but those parts by the big hotels are clean and safe.

▼ Juan Dolio beach scene

Sugar country

The coastal resorts come to an end with the large port city of **San Pedro de Macorís**, a sprawling metropolis of some 300 000 people. This hot and polluted place, badly battered by Hurricane Georges in 1998, is a shadow of its former self, its declining fortunes mirroring those of the country's beleaguered sugar industry. The city was once one of the wealthiest in the country, especially in the early part of the twentieth century when a post-World War I rise in sugar prices, coinciding with the US occupation and related investment, fuelled a brief boom. San Pedro was suddenly an important economic centre, with sugar factories, warehouses and workers' camps, known as *bateys*, spreading around the town. Railways connected the outlying sugar plantations to the mills nearer the town, while warehouses along the sluggish Higuamo River stored refined sugar for export to the US. A PanAm Clipper service connected San Pedro to the US, its seaplanes landing on the river mouth. There was even an opera house.

The labour force used to work the plantations was imported, with many cane-cutters coming from the impoverished small islands of the Eastern Caribbean. Thousands of English-speaking workers arrived from Anguilla, St Kitts and Nevis and Tortola, from which the corrupted word *cocolo* became their nickname. Working for a pittance and living in primitive *bateys*, the *cocolos* endured a good deal of hardship, but from the 1890s onwards a significant number settled permanently, bringing their language and religion with them. Most significantly perhaps, their skill at cricket was transformed into a natural talent for baseball, the sport which arrived with the Americans in 1916. Today, there are still descendants of these immigrants in San Pedro, playing a distinctive part in Christmas and local fiesta celebrations.

San Pedro is still predominantly a sugar town, the smoke from its mills hanging over the landscape. The once-ornate homes of the sugar barons are mostly in poor shape, and the waterside warehouses are decrepit, for the bottom fell out of the sugar industry decades ago. But the city's biggest mill, **Ingenio Porvenir**, remains in operation and can be visited. The neoclassical church of **San Pedro Apóstol**, built in 1911 and looking out onto the river, is a reminder of better times, as is the weirdly ornate fire station near the *Parque Central*, a piece of 1907 English design. Locals enjoy the broad *Malecón*, skirting the river and sea, and it is here that most activity and social life take place.

San Pedro's greatest export these days is its baseball players. A sign welcomes visitors to the city of sugar and *peloteros*, and it is clear that the two are interlinked, for it was out of the sugar plantations and dirt-poor *bateys* that a succession of world-class players emerged. The best-known is Sammy Sosa, but several San Pedro natives currently play at the highest level in the US, with the result that American – and Japanese – clubs have permanent scouting facilities in the region. The ugly modern **Tetelo Vargas stadium** is in the middle of town and offers an insight into the sport and the prospect of wealth and fame it holds out to poor but ambitious youths.

La Romana

Some 120 kilometres (75 miles) east of Santo Domingo is another coastal town where sugar has ruled supreme for a century or more. Smaller and wealthier than San Pedro, **La Romana** owes its comparative prosperity not just to one of the largest sugar complexes in the country, the **Central La Romana**, but also to the large-scale luxury resort of Casa de Campo a short distance to the east of the town.

The large Central Romana mill, with its huge smoking chimney, was established in 1917, only 20 years after the spread-out present-day town was established. It soon became one of the biggest sugar producing facilities in the Caribbean and after decades of ups and down was sold in 1967 to the US multinational company, Gulf & Western. The American firm invested heavily in the town, funding schools, hospitals and workers' housing, but critics claimed that it was an oppressive employer, outlawing unions and refusing pay negotiations. In the 1980s Gulf & Western sold up to a wealthy Cuban family based in Florida.

The sugar mill is a major source of employment, while thousands of Haitians toil in the plantations, some as temporary labourers and others as long-stay residents. The night-time hooting of trains carrying loads of cut cane to the factory is a constant reminder of sugar's importance. The other big employer is the free trade zone to the north of the town, a fenced off manufacturing complex where mostly female workers assemble clothing and electronic goods for export.

La Romana has little of architectural interest other than a few streets of turn-of-the-century houses around the *Parque Central*. Its main points of interest are outside the town, especially in the peculiar legacy left by Gulf & Western. One relic of the company's rule over the region is the huge **Casa de Campo** resort, built in 1974 on the whim of Gulf & Western's owner Charles Bluhdorn. The resort comprises 7000 acres of former sugar land that has been turned into a self-contained tropical paradise of beaches, luxuriant gardens, a world-class golf course, several restaurants and accommodation ranging from rooms to private villas. With rates of about $400 a night, the clientele is largely made up of celebrities such as Michael Jackson and Madonna. A marina at the mouth of the Río Chavón is aimed at wealthy yacht enthusiasts, while residents can play polo and tennis and ride horses. Many arrive via the resort's private airport.

This deluxe enclave is off-limits to non-guests, although the other Gulf & Western monument – which is, in any case, more interesting – is open to the public. This is the village of **Altos de Chavón**, occupying a dramatic plateau above the Casa de Campo with the Chavón River running below through a lush palm-filled valley. What is bizarre about

▲ Marina, La Romana

▲ Tuscany in the Caribbean

Altos de Chavón is that it is an idealised reconstruction of a sixteenth-century Tuscan village in the middle of the Dominican countryside. Cobbled streets, fountains and arcaded buildings made of specially aged stone all add to the illusion, though it is hard to forget that this Mediterranean forgery was built in the 1970s. A museum of Taino artefacts reminds visitors that they are in the Caribbean.

▲ The Chavón River

Artists are much in evidence in the village, which has several exhibition spaces, and there are hotel rooms, restaurants and craft shops. There is even an imitation open-air Roman amphitheatre, which can seat 7000 spectators. Julio Iglesias, who reportedly has financial interests in Casa de Campo, has performed there, as has Frank Sinatra. From the top of the plateau the views over the river are spectacular, though the complex itself is often filled with coach parties from visiting cruise ships.

▼ Altos de Chavón amphitheatre

The Parque Nacional del Este

The remote southeastern tip could hardly be more different from the well-trodden tourist alleyways of Altos de Chavón. Here, around the 430 square-kilometre (166 square-mile) **Parque Nacional del Este**, a handful of relaxed fishing villages are beginning to welcome visitors, many of whom are heading for the offshore island of Isla Saona. **Bayahibe**, situated on the western side of the park, is the most developed of these communities, and its prettily painted wooden houses look out onto the calm Caribbean Sea. Nearby, a cluster of all-inclusive resorts (**Club Viva Dominicus, Amhsa Casa del Mar, Coral Canoa Beach Hotel**) offer packages of immaculate beach, fine food and entertainment. To the east, the fishing village of **Boca de Yuma** has been less fortunate. The devastation wrought by Hurricane Georges in 1998 has yet to be cleared up, and restoration work is proceeding slowly.

▲ Bayahibe

The park itself is hot and dry, giving sanctuary to over 100 species of birds, rhinoceros iguanas and the rare solenodon and hutia mammals. Roads are non-existent, so visitors must take a boat ride from the beach at Bayahibe. This allows access to

various parts of the park, including the cave complex that can be reached by a rough track from the tiny settlement of **Peñon Gordo**. These underground chambers contain Taino petroglyphs, as do other more remote caves that can only be visited with a DNP guide.

The most popular attraction, however, is the less demanding **Isla Saona**, a tropical dream of white sands and coconut trees set within the park itself. There are a couple of small fishing villages on this 115 square-kilometre (44 square-mile) island, but most people are day-trippers from the resorts at Bávaro and Punta Cana who come on catamarans from Bayahibe to admire the beaches, the freshwater lagoons and the rum cocktails provided by tour operators. Critics have pointed out that large numbers of tourists are not consistent with the aims of a national park, but the island is big enough not to be spoiled by such excursions.

Less visited but of greater historic significance is a 500-year-old house near the inland town of **San Rafael del Yuma**. This fortified two-storey residence, strengthened with thick walls and tiny windows, was built by the Spanish conquistador Juan Ponce de León, the man who went on to conquer Puerto Rico and establish a Spanish settlement in Florida. From 1502 to 1508, he was governor of the eastern district of Higüey, sent to pacify rebellious Tainos, and it was with indigenous forced labour that his stout *forteleza* was built. The house was restored and re-roofed in 1997 but still contains several artefacts from Ponce de León's age, not least the bed in which he is said to have slept.

The coconut coast

An aerial photo of the 60-kilometre (37-mile) coastline that runs from Punta Cana up to Miches shows clearly why it is called the coconut coast. Miles and miles of pristine sand borders calm aquamarine water, the beaches framed by long lines of swaying coconut palms and thickets of sea grape. Inland, the palms continue, forming thick groves which eventually merge with the dry forest that carpets the plain. Sprinkled along this wild and remote coastline are a number of almost self-contained tourist resorts, large in scale and with every conceivable amenity.

The two biggest are **Punta Cana** and **Bávaro**. The Club Med at Punta Cana opened in 1981 and other all-inclusive hotel complexes, numbering their beds by the hundred, have sprung up since. They offer access to beautiful beaches

▲ Bávaro Beach   ▶ Beach sports

protected by coral reefs, a wide range of water sports, and an array of eating, drinking and self-pampering facilities. The **Bávaro Beach Resort**, for instance, contains five separate hotels, totalling around 2000 rooms, with nightclubs, casino and even a church. As the price paid in advance includes all food and drinks, there is less incentive for some visitors to leave the luxury of their complex and explore the more rough-and-ready country in the interior.

The formula seems to work, for some 750 000 people stay each year at the two main resorts. An airport at Punta Cana welcomes charters from North America and Europe and connecting flights from Santo Domingo. There is a more exclusive dimension to this region, too. At **Los Corales**, a fenced off collection of beachside mansions welcome magnates such as the Dominican designer Oscar de la Renta as well as A-list celebrities like Bill Clinton.

Outside the hotels there is little to do except walk the endless expanse of sand, visit an occasional beach bar or souvenir stand, or take a look at the spacious **Manatí Park** outside Bávaro, a cross between an aquarium and zoo, where dolphins perform tricks and dancing horses are put on show.

North of the resorts, the Costa del Coco stretches upwards until it becomes the southern coast of Samaná Bay. The beaches all along the coastline are spectacular and almost inevitably deserted but the water is rougher as one travels north and the roads to the sea are extremely poor. Two lagoons, the **Laguna Redondo** and

the **Laguna Limón**, have extensive mangrove forests, but cannot be reached without a four-wheel drive vehicle. Many different birds are to be seen here, as well as the sea turtles which lay their eggs on the wild beaches in the spring. The small town of **Miches** marks the beginning of the Samaná Bay. It is best-known these days as the departure point for the boats or *yolas* that cross the Mona Passage with their cargoes of illegal immigrants to Puerto Rico. Further west, the nondescript town of **Sabana de la Mar** is the departure point for boat trips to the **Parque Nacional de los Haitises**, a protected expanse of mangrove swamps, bumpy hills known as *mogotes* and dense tropical vegetation. This remote part of the country has so far avoided development, and so the park contains a rich array of ecological interest as well as Taino-decorated caves that can be visited only by boat and with a guide from Sabana de la Mar.

Higüey and the interior

In from the coast, the eastern part of the Dominican Republic is a land of large sugar plantations, isolated villages and small market towns. Places such as Hato Mayor are isolated communities, with little to interest the tourist, but typical of a rural Dominican *pueblo*. A mix of one-storey wooden houses and more modern concrete dwellings line a grid of dusty, often unmade streets, with the *Parque Central* the focus of the town. Corner stores/bars provide meeting places, as do plazas and other open spaces where children play baseball. Towns like this are transport hubs, shopping centres for outlying districts, and home to people who either work in the surrounding farms or in stores and offices. Where once there were only horses and cattle, there is now a bustling commotion of buses and *motoconchos*.

The nearest town of any size to the Costa del Coco mega-resorts is **Higüey**, a hot and dusty metropolis of 150 000 people, which serves as the main commercial centre for the agricultural interior of the eastern Dominican Republic. Founded in 1494 and the power base of Ponce de León, it has little left from that period. Instead, it has a large market, full of fruit and vegetables, which occupies several congested streets, and a *motoconcho*-infested town centre with few buildings of distinction. Its one architectural attraction, however, is famous throughout the country as the nation's most revered holy site and a place of pilgrimage.

The huge concrete **Basílica de Nuestra Señora de la Altagracia** is unmissable, as it towers over the city and can be seen from all around. It commemorates a miraculous appearance by the Virgin (and patron saint of the Republic) who in the seventeenth century cured a sick girl. A pilgrimage became established in 1922 when

▲ Higüey Cathedral

the Virgin became the national patron saint and every year on 21 January, thousands of Dominicans file past a glass-covered image of the saint in the hope of their own miracle.

The pilgrimage initially centred around Higüey's sixteenth-century San Dionisio church, but Trujillo wanted something altogether more monumental to symbolise a truly national expression of faith. The result is the 80-metre (267 feet) high concrete basilica, designed by two French architects in the 1950s and finally finished in 1971. Its unabashed modernism appeals to some, and its mix of curves, arches and towering spire in the form of a curving loop is certainly memorable, but many visitors dislike it. Its controversial appearance does little, however, to deter the throngs of faithful every January.

⑨ Border country
The southwest

The southwest contains the Dominican Republic's badlands – hot, dry desert studded with cactus and thorny scrub where only lizards and iguanas can survive the burning heat. Its wild extremes also include a high mountain range, a long and largely empty coastline and one of the country's greatest natural curiosities – a large inland expanse of salt water populated by crocodiles. The region has long been the poorest in the country, and many small towns and villages are noticeably less developed and prosperous than elsewhere. In this sense, it begins to mirror conditions across the border in Haiti, the poorest nation in the Western hemisphere.

This part of the Dominican Republic is deeply marked by its proximity to Haiti. Towns were created or destroyed by Haitian invaders in the nineteenth century, while battles were fought across the region. Tens of thousands of Haitian migrants come across the border every year in search of work and a better life, and many of them remain in the agricultural areas around the town of Barahona, where poverty-stricken *bateys* are home to communities of cane-cutters and their families. The bustling border towns of Jimaní and Elias Piña hold regular markets at which goods and people cross to and fro across the porous frontier.

But it is the natural beauty of the southwest that is drawing a wealthier class of visitor from North America and Europe, as it gradually opens up to tourism. This is not the mass tourism of the north or east coasts, and as yet there are few all-inclusive resorts or crowded beaches. Instead, visitors here are more interested in eco-tourism, in exploring still remote wildernesses and undeveloped coastlines.

San Cristóbal

The well-maintained Carretera Sánchez (Highway 2) quickly leaves Santo Domingo's western suburbs behind, passing the industrial port of Haina and the chimneys of the town's large sugar mill, and heads into flat sugar land. The first big town is the provincial capital of **San Cristóbal**, a sprawling and unattractive place of almost 200 000 inhabitants. It was here that the Dominican Republic's first constitution, in 1844, was signed. But

◀ San Cristóbal

its main claim to fame, or notoriety, is that the dictator Trujillo was born here and lavished much money on his beloved hometown. The most obvious result is the large, mustard-coloured cathedral, a disproportionately grandiose structure topped by white angels and boasting a Byzantine-style dome. Trujillo reputedly wanted to be buried here in a lavish crypt and for this reason spent the extravagant sum of $4 million on the cathedral's construction in 1946. It contains Biblical murals by José Vela Zanetti as well as mahogany pews and altar. Outside, a renovated plaza has palm trees and fountains – but no water.

Further reminders of the dictator's megalomania are to be found around the town that he renamed 'meritorious city' in his own honour. The monstrous **El Cerro** mansion sits on a hill looking over San Cristóbal, six semi-circular floors of crumbling concrete that was once lined with mahogany and gold plate. So extravagant was this palace that when Trujillo asked a European ambassador for his opinion, the undiplomatic diplomat replied that it was tasteless. A wounded Trujillo never lived there after this rebuke. This ugly building is supposed to have been renovated but looks abandoned. A few fading murals by Vanetti can still be made out.

▲ El Cerro

More tasteful is the *Generalísimo's* other San Cristóbal residence, the **Casa de Caoba** (Mahogany House), placed on a wooded hilltop some 3 kilometres (2 miles) north of town. This country retreat was a greater success than El Cerro, and Trujillo spent much time here (often with one of his many mistresses). It was originally built almost entirely of the rare and expensive hardwood, but years of neglect after Trujillo's death caused the plainly designed house to rot, and restoration was half-hearted and clumsy. In 2000, the government announced that both buildings would be thoroughly restored, the Casa de Caoba as a museum and testament to Trujillo's tyranny.

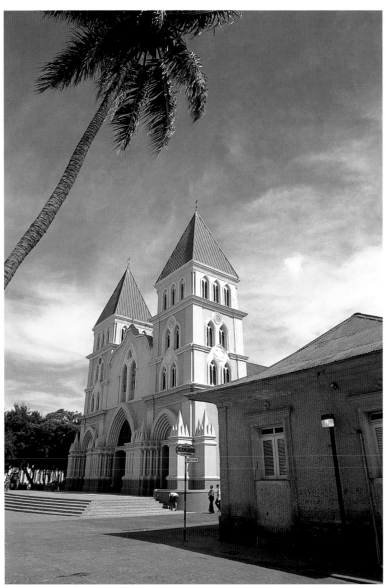

▲ San Cristóbal's cathedral

The road north out of San Cristóbal leads on another 12 kilometres (8 miles) past the Mahogany House to a *balneario* or freshwater swimming hole (actually a number of pools) called **La Toma**. Trujillo apparently enjoyed an occasional dip here, and a small entrance fee allows visitors to enjoy the cool waters of the Haina River. Almost adjacent is the entrance to the **El Pomier Archaeological Reserve**, a complex of 54 caves filled with Taino petroglyphs. A long walk from the gates of the reserve takes you to three large and easily accessible caverns (El Pomier) where hundreds of faint but visible charcoal images depict everyday scenes of animals and religious rites. Other caves in the network are off-limit, and El Pomier must be visited with an official guide. This expedition is not recommended for those with a fear of bats; there are thousands in the caves, as well as stalagmites and stalactites. Limestone mining has threatened this unique complex, but the government has recently pledged to protect it.

South of Trujillo's dusty hometown, sugar fields stretch gently towards the coast, where there are some popular beaches at **Najayo** and **Palenque**. The road running along the coast in fact avoids much of San Cristóbal, passing old sugar mills and then the grey sand of the two small resorts. Another ruined Trujillo mansion overlooks the beach at Najayo.

Baní and Azua

Sugarcane dominates the flat coastal landscape as the Carretera Sánchez stretches westwards away from the capital. **Baní**, a surprisingly prosperous town of some 100 000 people, is the next conurbation, sitting in a hot but fertile plain. The present-day town was settled in the eighteenth century by migrants from the Canary Islands, developing a reputation for hard work and economic success. A catastrophic fire in 1882 levelled most of the town, but it was rebuilt in Victorian style with some pretty ironwork and roof tiles. The town is the birthplace of Máximo Gómez (1836-1905), a key figure in the fight for Cuba's independence from Spain, and there is a modest museum and a pleasant park dedicated to the legendary liberation fighter. The town is also reputed as a centre of baseball excellence.

Baní's relative prosperity these days is due to coffee cultivation in the nearby mountains, other agriculture and salt extraction. This industry is located on the Las Salinas peninsula to the south of the town, where huge salt pans and mountains of white powder seem blindingly bright under the intense sun. Passing by the small naval base at **Las Calderas**, one sees extensive sand dunes to one's left, while to the right the large and placid **Bahía de Ocoa** shimmers against a background of hills and distant

▲ Baní

mountains. The village of **Las Salinas** has a hotel, seafood restaurants and a windsurfing club.

▲ Las Salinas

Between Baní and Azua a right turn up Highway 41 leads some 30 kilometres (19 miles) to the mountain town of **San José de Ocoa**, an undistinguished farming settlement set in a beautiful and cool environment on the southern edge of the Cordillera Central. This town is popular with people from Santo Domingo, keen to swim in its nearby *balnearios* and to enjoy the mountain scenery but sees few foreign visitors. The road up from the Sánchez highway is an experience in itself, winding through small farms and rugged mountain vistas.

If Baní is a relatively young town, **Azua**, about 40 kilometres (25 miles) further west and separated by the low mountain range of the Sierra El Número, is ancient, dating back to 1504. As an early Spanish settlement, it was home to Hernán Cortés, who worked for a while as its mayor and legal authority before setting off to conquer Mexico. Another *conquistador*, Diego Velásquez, was responsible for the initial founding of the town and later sailed to colonise Cuba. Juan Ponce de León was another resident with colonising ambitions; he established the first Spanish toehold in Florida after taking control of Puerto Rico.

Next to nothing remains from that early period, as Azua lay in the middle of the territory that was fought over between Haitians and Dominicans in 1844. Not only were the wooden houses burnt down by the retreating Haitians, but a number of earthquakes had already ensured the disappearance of any ancient structures. As a result, modern-day Azua is a mostly concrete town, placed in one of the Dominican Republic's hottest areas. Always busy with passing buses and *motoconchos*, its main streets are like those of any other Dominican market town, but even more congested. The first site of the town, on the coast, is now known as Puerto Viejo, but there is nothing to be seen of what was once an important port. South of the town are several fine beaches, notably the **Playa Blanca**.

Towards the border

To the west of Azua there are two roads to the Haitian border. Turning inland, a paved highway runs through rolling hills and farming villages to the frontier town of Elias Piña. Two towns are on this little-used road, San Juan de la Maguana and Las Matas de Farfán. This district was among those worst affected by Hurricane Georges in 1998, when several villages were destroyed and many lives were lost in landslides. **San Juan** is an unexpectedly large town with a rather monumental feel, an impression encouraged by a small version of the Arc de Triomphe at its entrance, large public buildings and some pleasant parks filled with statues and fountains. Essentially the commercial centre for an agricultural area, San Juan, whose name is a hybrid reference to St John the Baptist and the indigenous Taino Maguana people, has few touristy pretensions. It, like Azua, was demolished during the Haitian-Dominican conflict in the 1840s, and many of its people can claim some descent from eighteenth-century Canary Island immigrants.

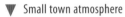 Small town atmosphere

▲ Market day at Elias Piña

Another 30 kilometres (19 miles) westwards lies the much smaller town of **Las Matas de Farfán**, the last place of any size before the border. Its best feature is its leafy *Parque Central*, decorated by a gazebo, but otherwise it has little of interest. From here it is only a half-hour drive to **Elias Piña**, a town that bustles with activity each Monday and Friday when hundreds of Haitian market traders cross the border with wares of all descriptions. The streets running towards the crossing point from the *Parque Central* are filled with tarpaulin-covered stalls, selling everything from second-hand shoes to bunches of bananas.

Foreigners are, in theory, not allowed to cross into Haiti at Elias Piña, but the adventurous can pay a small 'tip' to border officials and set foot in the Haitian town of Belladère, an even dustier version of its Dominican equivalent. There is little to see there, and after crossing the desolate no man's land that separates the two nations, a bumpy ride on a motorcycle taxi is essential to reach Belladère. No vehicles are allowed to cross. Given that Belladère has been the scene of politically motivated murders and alleged guerrilla activity in recent times, it is sensible to seek advice locally before crossing.

▲ Empty road near the Haitian border

Barahona and beyond

Back on the coastal plain, the other road towards Haiti heads southwards through dry and desert-like terrain, skirting the large **Bahía de Neiba**, a calm expanse of sea famous for its manatee population. This road is now the Highway 44, passing through cactus-studded hillsides and ramshackle villages, clearly poorer than elsewhere in the country. Amidst the rocky landscape a blaze of green announces the irrigation system fed by the waters of the Río Yaque del Sur and large banana plantations lining the road. Soon afterwards the road reaches **Barahona**.

▲ Barahona; cutting sugar cane

The biggest town in the remote southwest, with a population of around 100 000, Barahona was not established until 1802, when the area was under the control of the Haitian slave general, Toussaint Louverture. Toussaint saw the economic potential of an area rich in tropical woods, and the port developed as an export conduit for mahogany and other types of lumber. It is still a port, and rusting cargo ships can be seen loading up locally mined gypsum. Sugar is the other mainstay of the area, plantations and slum-like *bateys* surrounding the town. Despite the building of an international airport, named after a local beauty, María Montez, who became a 1940s movie star in the US, mass tourism is as yet still a dream.

The focal point of this grid-system town is the seaside *Malecón*, where hotels and restaurants are to be found. A couple of blocks inland is the *Parque Central*, where locals tend to congregate around the main post office. Elsewhere, the central streets buzz with *motoconchos* and the bustle of everyday commerce. There are many Haitians and Dominicans of Haitian descent in the town and around, and you can expect to hear Haitian Creole spoken as well as Spanish.

Barahona is not a beautiful place, but it acts as an excellent base for exploring the remote beaches to the southwest and the spectacular countryside around the Haitian border. The coastal road down to Oviedo runs along some of the most unspoilt scenery in the country, with rugged, forested mountains meeting empty and wild beaches. Occasional villages and small towns break the illusion of wilderness, but they are few and far between. Coming out of Barahona, one passes the village of **Arroyo**, where larimar, a semi-precious turquoise stone, is collected in makeshift open-cast mines. Visitors can view the mines up a dirt track and buy specimens at knock-down prices. Thereafter, the fishing villages of **San Rafael**, **Paraiso** and **Los Patos** offer little in the way of facilities (except on weekends when the beaches are filled with locals) but superb views out to sea and up into the hills.

▲ South of Barahona

▲ Los Patos

The hot desert-like settlement of **Oviedo** marks the gateway to the **Jaragua National Park**, the biggest and most inhospitable in the Republic. An almost untouched paradise for birds and reptiles, this vast expanse of limestone hills, cacti and tough scrub covers not just the bottom of the Pedernales Peninsula but two offshore islands and a large saltwater lagoon that shelters flamingos, frigate birds and pelicans. The park can only be explored with an official guide, to be found at the ranger station on the road before Oviedo itself.

From Oviedo to Pedernales, a fishing village and border post, the road turns inland, passing through 50 kilometres (31 miles) of arid and mostly uninhabited countryside where cacti grow high.

The Jaragua National Park is to the left, the mountains of the Sierra de Baoruco to the right. Here, too, is another national park, famous for its virgin pine forests and wide range of orchids. This is probably the most inaccessible of all the parks, and cannot be reached from the south. Easier to find are the beaches in and around Pedernales, including **Cabo Rojo** and the spectacularly wild **Bahía de las Aguilas**. This last beach, named after the eagles that Columbus believed he saw (they were more likely to have been buzzards), is earmarked for development by the government despite its position within the Jaragua National Park.

Pedernales has the desolate feel of a border town, and smuggling is reputed to be big business here, especially since the Alcoa bauxite operation closed down. But it has a pleasant beach and from here it is easy to negotiate with officials at the relaxed border post (where thousands of Haitians cross each year in search of work) and cross the stream that divides the two nations. The Haitian village of Anse-à-Pitres is directly across the frontier and easily accessible by motorcycle taxi. There is little to see, however, other than a littered beach, fishing boats and some poor palm-thatched houses.

Lago Enriquillo

The ghost of the legendary Taino chieftain, Enriquillo, is much in evidence in the southwest. The orphaned son of a murdered Taino leader, he was educated in Santo Domingo by the Spanish but rebelled against the colonial system, leading his indigenous followers into the impregnable mountains of the Sierra de Bahoruco. The revolt lasted from 1519 to 1533 as he launched guerrilla attacks on the Spanish. Eventually a peace treaty was signed, and Enriquillo was granted a residence near Azua, were he died two years later, probably of tuberculosis. The memory of the Taino chieftain is preserved in a coastal town of the same name, a statue near the lake at Rincón, and another, bigger lake – the **Lago Enriquillo**.

The lake is easily reached from Barahona after a drive that takes the visitor through some of the Dominican Republic's most scenic countryside. Passing through sugarcane plantations and the *bateys* attached to them, the road reaches the town of Galván, a centre for banana cultivation. From there it is a straight westward drive through lush banana fields to **La Descubierta**, a village situated on the shore of Lago Enriquillo. Ahead are the mountains that separate the Dominican Republic from Haiti. Just before the village, at a place called **Postrer Río**, is a complex of caves where Enriquillo is said to have hidden during his insurgency. The caves can be visited and contain carved images of indigenous faces (hence their name, Las Caritas or 'little faces').

From the National Park station to the east of La Descubierta it is easy to book a boat trip on the lake to visit the island in its middle. The lake itself is vast (200 square kilometres [77 square miles]) and sits almost 50 metres (164 feet) below sea level. It was once linked to the Bahía de Neiba, but was then cut off from the sea by earth-shifting tectonic activity around a million years ago. The water is three times saltier than the sea, despite several rivers flowing into the lake, and the surrounding shorelines as well as the island are littered with ancient coral and sea shells. The lake, three islands and surrounding land comprise the **Parque Nacional Isla Cabritos**, established as a sanctuary in 1966.

The lake can look slightly sinister, with dead trees protruding from the water and rather bleak sun-baked surrounds, but the main attraction is the **Isla Cabritos** (Goat Island), a flat 12-kilometre (7-mile) long patch of sand and scrub in the lake. This unwelcoming place is home to large (and alarmingly tame) iguanas, flamingos and turtles. Most exciting of all – through hard to spot after the early morning – are the American crocodiles that lay their eggs on the island. These shy and harmless beasts tend to prefer the northwestern end of the lake during the day, as it is here that fresh water and food enter the salty lake.

The boat trip takes parties of visitors to the island, where iguanas approach in the hope of a treat, and then rangers or guides try to locate a crocodile or two for a photo opportunity, sometimes leaping into the shallow water to push a reluctant croc nearer the boat. The trip is exceedingly hot and should be avoided during the middle of the day.

The lake can be circled by car, and it is worth driving around its southern shore when returning to Barahona or Santo Domingo. This circuit takes you to the border town of **Jimaní**, another crossing point into Haiti and one of two official border exits for foreigners (the other is Dajabón). Like the other frontier communities, its main raison d'être is the two-way flow of Haitian migrants and smuggled goods (including, so it is said, Colombian cocaine). More visible is the Haitian market, just beyond the border post, on a scorched wasteland. On offer are fake designer brands, Haitian rum and improbably large piles of pots and pans. Should you wish to enter Haiti here, it is a 5-kilometre (3-mile) drive out of Jimaní itself to a crossing point where departure and entrance taxes are payable (you are not allowed to take a hire car across, and foreigners are viewed as fair game by bribe-happy officials). As for Jimaní itself, it is a spread-out community of single-storey concrete buildings, with temperatures sometimes exceeding 50°C.

Returning to Barahona, one sees the modern statue of Enriquillo at a road junction near Duvergé. Soon after, the country's second biggest lake, the **Laguna de Rincón**, comes into view. This 47 square-kilometre (18 square-mile) freshwater lagoon can only be reached by a dirt track from the town of **Cabral**, but birdwatchers will be rewarded with sightings of local species of duck and heron.

From Cabral it is worth taking a diversion up a road leading to **Polo**. As the road climbs, the views of the lake and surrounding mountains are stunning. There is also one of the country's unsolved mysteries to be investigated here. At one point the road appears to run uphill, but if a car is left in neutral or a ball placed on the road it will roll upwards. Scientists have concluded that the phenomenon of the 'Polo Magnético' is no more than an optical illusion, but some prefer a more esoteric explanation, based on Taino spirits or underground energy forces. The road continues upwards into cooler mountain terrain, ideal for coffee cultivation. In the friendly village of Polo, marking the end of the road, you can see coffee beans lying on tarpaulins under the drying rays of the sun.

▶ Enriquillo

A–Z of facts and information

Air links

As a major Caribbean hub, the Dominican Republic is well served by regular flights from North America, Europe and the rest of the Caribbean. American Airlines (www.aa.com) flies from New York and Miami, Continental (www.continental.com) from Newark, and TWA (www.twa.com) from New York. Canadian Airlines (www.cdnair.ca) flies from Toronto and Montreal. American Eagle (www.aa.com) links the Dominican Republic to Puerto Rico, and Cubana (www.cubana.cu) runs a service to and from Cuba. From Europe there are scheduled services from Paris (Air France, www.airfrance.com) and Madrid (Iberia, www.iberia.com). There are also a great many charters from North America and Europe. Fares are highest around Christmas time, when many Dominicans return home. The main airport is Las Américas, but local flights and charters also land in Puerto Plata, Punta Cana, La Romana and Barahona.

Banks

Banks tend to be open from 8.30AM to 3.30PM, Monday to Friday. There are several chains of banks throughout the country such as Baninter and Banco Popular where traveller's cheques can be cashed and cash advances received against Visa and other credit cards. ATMs are now fairly common, but sometimes do not work or are soon emptied at weekends. Expect long, slow moving queues at banks, but it is safer and better value to change currency here than anywhere else.

Car hire

Most international agencies such as Avis and Hertz operate in the Dominican Republic, especially in tourist resorts. Car rental is not cheap, and it does not make sense to use cheaper companies, whose vehicles can be suspect. The minimum age for hiring a car is 25 and a valid licence is required. A hefty deposit will be required. It is essential to have adequate insurance, as Dominican driving can be erratic. Remember to drive on the right, to avoid using a car at night, and to watch out for humans and animals on country roads.

Dress

Dominicans dress smartly, even when poor, and do not appreciate over-casual visitors. Beachwear is for the beach only, and shorts should not be worn if visiting churches. Hotels are more relaxed about dress code than traditional restaurants, where a jacket is expected for men. Implausible as it may seem, it is recommended that visitors to the higher regions of the Cordillera Central take a sweater or some item of warm clothing. Clothes are cheap to buy.

Emergencies

The national emergency phone number is 911, connecting to police and fire and medical services. Most hotels will have a local doctor on call. Private insurance is indispensable to receive good-quality health care in a properly resourced hospital. In case of serious problems, embassy details are as follows:

UK Embassy: Avenida 27 de Febrero 233, Santo Domingo, tel (809) 472 7111/7671

US Embassy: César Nicolás Pensón, Esq. Máximo Gómez, Santo Domingo, tel (809) 221 5511

Faiths

Although Roman Catholicism is the majority religion, there are many other faiths and churches represented, from Baptists to Bahá'í. The Episcopal Church on Avenida Independencia 253, Santo Domingo, has a Sunday morning service in English.

Guaguas

The common name for the beaten-up vans that form an unregulated transport network throughout the Dominican Republic. Normally connecting towns and villages along a fixed route, they hold around six passengers and are an excellent way of meeting Dominicans. They are also extremely frequent and cheap (although you should always establish the cost of a journey before setting off). They leave from major intersections and can be waved down (the destination will be shown in the front window).

Health

Vaccinations are not normally required, though it is sensible to boost tetanus and to consider hepatitis A and B jabs. Rabies exists, and any worrying contact with a wild animal or dog should be reported at once. Malaria is present near the Haitian border, and it makes sense to take a course of prophylactics and to avoid mosquito bites as much as possible. Dengue fever is less dangerous but also mosquito-transmitted. The main risks to ordinary travellers are sunburn and an upset stomach, both of which can be avoided by precautions. Avoid the midday sun and do not drink tap water or drinks with ice that may not be purified. It is normally wise to eat only food that is freshly cooked (i.e. not luke-warm buffet meals). HIV and Aids are both prevalent.

Information

Good internet sources of information include:
News: www.dr1.com (in English)
News: www.listin.com.do (Spanish-language online edition of Santo Domingo's best daily)
Tourism: www.turinter.com (local tour operator)
Food and drink: www.dominicancooking.com (in English)
General: www.lanic.utexas.edu (portal for Latin American/Caribbean sites)

Jewellery

The country is famous for relatively inexpensive jewellery featuring amber and larimar, both of which are mined locally. This makes a good present or souvenir. Pieces of untreated amber and larimar can be bought very cheaply, but it is also good value to shop at one of the more reputable stores in Santo Domingo or Puerto Plata (e.g. Harrison's). Do not buy amber from street touts, as it is fake.

▲ Puerto Plata's Amber Museum

▲ Snail mail Dominican style

Keeping in touch

Thanks to a modern telecommunications network, it is easy to make phone calls to North America and Europe. These can be made at Codetel offices in every town or (more expensively) from hotels. One option is to buy a Codetel phone card (sold in denominations of RD$75 to RD$500), which can be used in public phone boxes for international as well as local calls. Codetel's main competitor, Tricom, also has public phones. Calls are much cheaper after 6PM and at weekends. The postal service is slow and extremely unreliable. Codetel offices offer internet access (which is often down) and there are new internet cafés in Santo Domingo and the tourist resorts.

Lavatories

Public toilets are a rare luxury in the Dominican Republic, and those that exist are not normally attractive. All decent hotels have good facilities, as do restaurants and some long-distance buses. Remember to have toilet paper available when out and about.

Money

The Dominican currency is the peso (RD$), divided into 100 centavos. Notes range from 5 to 1000 pesos (although the latter is hard to change). The peso varies in value against the US dollar and has tended to depreciate since it was allowed to 'float' freely in the 1990s. Dollars are accepted (as are credit cards) in tourist venues but often at a poor rate of exchange. You should never try to exchange money on the street or in any other form of black market context, as hustlers invariably try to cheat you.

National parks

The Dirección Nacional de Parques (DNP), a government agency, is in charge of 70 areas of special natural or scientific interest and issues permits to enter the various national parks. Permits can be obtained at offices attached to the parks or the main office can be visited in Santo Domingo next door to the zoo on Avenida Máximo Gómez (tel, (809) 472 4204). Opening times are 08.00 to 15.00, and permits cost around $4 (£2.50).

Outdoor activities

Apart from water sports, the main centres for cycling, riding, hiking and canyoning are listed below. Both are recommended as knowledgeable and security-conscious:
Iguana Mama, Cabarete, tel (809) 571 0908,
www.iguanamama.com
Rancho Baiguate, Jarabacoa, tel (809) 574 6890,
www.ranchobaiguate,com.do
Aventuras del Caribe, La Vega, tel (809) 242 0395 www.dr-canyon.com

Public holidays and festivals

New Year's Day (1 January), Epiphany (6 January), Our Lady of Altagracia (21 January), Duarte Day (26 January), Independence Day (27 February), Good Friday, Labour Day (1 May), Corpus Christi (60 days after Good Friday), Restoration Day (16 August),

All Saints' Day (1 November), Christmas Day (25 December).

Some public holidays coincide with weekends, in which case most Dominicans take an extended break, especially around Holy Week. Apart from the saint's day celebrated by almost every community, the big festivals are 21 January, when a pilgrimage to the cathedral at Higüey is accompanied by parades and parties at many other locales, Carnival (end of February, with huge out-door events on Santo Domingo's *Malecón*) and the July Merengue Festival.

Quincentenary

The five hundredth anniversary of Christopher Columbus' arrival in and naming of Hispaniola was the pretext for a huge amount of restoration work in the capital's *zona colonial* as well as the controversial Faro a Colón (Columbus Lighthouse) on the other side of the Ozama River. The event took place on 12 October 1992 (although this was the date of his landing in The Bahamas) and was particularly supported by the government of the late Joaquín Balaguer. Whether we view Columbus as an intrepid discoverer or a gold-mad adventurer, it is clear that the anniversary did much to transform the most historically fascinating area of Santo Domingo.

Rum

Along with jewellery and cigars, rum is one of the country's best exports and souvenirs. Three brands, Barceló, Brugal and Bermúdez compete for market share, and as a general rule the older the rum the better and mellower its taste. 'Añejo' is the generic term for rums aged in oak barrels. Both the Brugal distillery in Puerto Plata and the Bermúdez installation in Santiago welcome visitors and offer free samples.

Shopping

There are shops of every description, from Santo Domingo's US-style malls to tiny and atmospheric corner grocery stores in every village. Apart from rum, cigars and semi-precious stones, foreign visitors are attracted by art (much of it mass-produced across the border in Haiti but still very colourful) and music. Most tourist areas have stores devoted to satisfying these consumer needs, but much better bargains are to be had by the more adventurous visitor who ventures into Santo Domingo's Avenida Mella/Mercado Modelo district or the main market in Puerto Plata. Haggling is acceptable in markets where, in any case, you are liable to be charged above the going local rate but not in shops. Make sure when using credit cards that you are signing in RD$ and not US$ (a common con trick in less reputable outlets).

▲ Shopping on the beach

Taxes

A departure tax of US$10 is payable per head at airports. There are many other indirect taxes levied on tourists: a 23 per cent tax on hotel rooms, 8 per cent on food and drink, and 10 per cent on restaurant meals. None of these applies to all-inclusive packages. Tipping is also expected in restaurants.

United States

Dominican history from the early nineteenth century onwards has been dramatically influenced by the country's proximity to the US. Not only did the independent nation's leaders try to sell or lease parts of the territory to the US, but they also tried to become a full-fledged State – without success. Despite two occupations by US Marines, most Dominicans are very well disposed towards America and Americans, to the point where large numbers each year seek to join, legally or illegally, the estimated million Dominicans living and working in the US. American influence is evident in all walks of life, from fast food and baseball to the constitution, and this cultural intermixing is reinforced by the steady stream of Dominicans to and from New York and other US cities.

Visas

US, Canadian, British and all European Union citizens must have a valid passport, a return ticket and a 90-day tourist card (cost US$10) in order to enter the Dominican Republic. The card can be obtained upon arrival. If you wish to stay beyond 90 days, you have to renew the card for a further 90 days (again US$10) at the airport immigration office. Permanent residence and/or work permits are very hard and expensive to obtain. The first step is to contact the relevant Dominican consulate.

Women travellers

Women travellers on their own (or even in groups) can expect a good deal of unwanted attention from Dominican *macho* men. A minor annoyance rather than a real treat, this involves exaggerated compliments and persistence. It is wise, however, not to frequent deserted beaches or empty streets at night. Most men, it should be said, are courteous and considerate.

X

Marks the spot where buried or submerged treasure is supposed to be hidden. There are many wrecks of Spanish galleons and pirate treasure ships lying in waters around the Dominican coast as well as reputed hoards of buried treasure inland. Some diving companies specialise in visiting such sites. See www.treasurenet.com

Young visitors

Most Dominicans are very friendly and welcoming towards children, and contact with ordinary people is often made much easier by the presence of a child. All-inclusives may be the best option for those with young children, as they offer entertainments and even baby-sitting facilities. Children should be especially protected from the harmful effects of the tropical sun and should avoid tap water and potentially unclean ice.

Zoos

There is a surprisingly good zoo in Santo Domingo, complete with landscaped gardens and a shuttle train. An African enclosure is interesting, as are examples of rare domestic mammals. Avenida de los Reyes Católicos, tel (809) 562 3149.

Bibliography

Non-fiction

Emelio Betances, *State and Society in the Dominican Republic* (Westview Press, Boulder CO, 1995) An academic but readable analysis of the relationship between political and economic power.

James Ferguson, *Traveller's History of the Caribbean* (Interlink, New York, 1998) Concise history of the region and the role of the Dominican Republic.

Harry Hoetink, *The Dominican People* (Johns Hopkins University Press, Baltimore, 1982) Fascinating detail on where the country's culturally mixed population comes from and how its immigrants arrived.

David Howard, *Coloring the Nation: Race and Ethnicity in the Dominican Republic* (Signal Books/Lynne Rienner, Oxford/Boulder CO, 2001) Looks at troubled relations between the Dominican Republic and Haiti and analyses the Dominican obsession with race.

David Howard, *Dominican Republic in Focus* (Latin America Bureau/Interlink Books, London/New York, 1998) Very useful short introduction, covering everything from Columbus to bachata.

Frank Moya Pons, *The Dominican Republic: A National History* (Hispaniola Books, New York, 1994) An accessible history of the country by its foremost contemporary historian.

Michele Wucker, *Why the Cocks Fight: Dominicans, Haitians, and the Struggle for Hispaniola* (Hill and Wang, New York, 1999) Vivid account of why the divided island has created so much hatred.

Fiction

Julia Alvarez, *How the Garcia Girls Lost Their Accent* (Plume-Penguin, New York, 1991) A perceptive story of a Dominican family caught between the US and *la isla*.

Julia Alvarez, *In the Time of the Butterflies* (Algonquin Books, Chapel Hill NC, 1994) The horrors of the Trujillo period skilfully brought to life in a (real-life) tale of murder and heroism.

Junot Díaz, *Drown* (Faber & Faber, London, 1996) Tough and gritty short stories from the barrios of New Jersey and the Dominican villages left behind by the emigrants.

Manuel de Jesús Galván, *Enriquillo* (1889) (*The Cross and the Sword*, Victor Gollancz, London, 1956) The classic story of the Taino *cacique* and his impossible revolt against Spanish colonial rule.

Pamela Maria Smorkaloff, *If I Could Write This in Fire: An Anthology of Writing from the Caribbean* (New Press, New York, 1994) Excellent anthology, including work by the Dominican Republic's 'national poet', Pedro Mir.

Also available in the MACMILLAN CARIBBEAN GUIDES SERIES

Anguilla: Tranquil Isle of the Caribbean – Brenda Carty and Colville Petty

Antigua and Barbuda: Heart of the Caribbean – Brian Dyde

The Bahamas: Family of Islands – Gail Saunders

Barbados: The Visitors' Guide – F A Hoyos

Belize: Ecotourism in Action – Meb Cutlack

The Islands of Bermuda: Another World – David Raine

Dominica: Isle of Adventure – Lennox Honychurch

Grenada: Isle of Spice – Norma Sinclair

Jamaica: The Fairest Isle – Philip Sherlock and Barbara Preston

Nevis: Queen of the Caribees – Joyce Gordon

St Kitts: Cradle of the Caribbean – Brian Dyde

St Lucia: Helen of the West Indies – Guy Ellis

St Vincent and the Grenadines – Lesley Sutty

Tobago: An Introduction and Guide – Eaulin Blondel

The Turks and Caicos Islands: Lands of Discovery – Amelia Smithers and Anthony Taylor

USVI: America's Virgin Islands – Arlene Martel